Harcourt Health and Fitness

Teaching Resources
Grade 6

Harcourt
SCHOOL PUBLISHERS

Orlando • Austin • New York • San Diego • Toronto • London

Visit *The Learning Site!*
www.harcourtschool.com

Photo Credits

All other photos © Harcourt School Publishers.

Grateful acknowledgment is made to the Partnership for Food Safety Education for permission to reprint Fight BAC! information graphic. Copyright 2003 by Partnership for Food Safety Education.

Printed in the United States of America

ISBN 0-15-339090-5

1 2 3 4 5 6 7 8 9 10 054 13 12 11 10 09 08 07 06 05 04

Contents

Health Resources

School–Home Connection Letters

Writing Models

Contents (Continued)

Organizers

Resources for the Coordinated School Health Program

CSHP This directory lists agencies that provide support for the eight different aspects of the Coordinated School Health Program and will aid you in your classroom planning and teaching activities. While every effort has been made to provide complete and accurate website addresses, the nature of the World Wide Web makes it impossible to follow every link on every site to ensure reliable and up-to-date information. Please use your own discretion about the suitability of the material found on a site, and preview any site to which you refer your students.

Advocates for Youth
1025 Vermont Ave., NW, Suite 210
Washington, DC 20005
Phone: (202) 347-5700
Fax: (202) 347-2263
http://www.advocatesforyouth.org

American Academy of Child & Adolescent Psychiatry
3615 Wisconsin Ave., NW
Washington, DC 20016-3007
Phone: (202) 966-7300
Fax: (202) 966-2891
http://www.aacap.org

American Academy of Pediatrics
141 Northwest Point Blvd.
Elk Grove Village, IL 60007
Phone: (847) 434-4000
Fax: (847) 434-8000
http://www.aap.org

American Association for Active Lifestyles & Fitness
1900 Association Dr.
Reston, VA 22091
Phone: (800) 213-7193
Fax: (703) 476-9527
http://www.aahperd.org/aaalf/aaalfmain.html

American Association for Health Education
1900 Association Dr.
Reston, VA 22091
Phone: (703) 476-3437
Fax: (703) 476-6638
http://www.aahperd.org/aahe/aahemain.html

American Association of School Administrators
1801 N. Moore St.
Arlington, VA 22209
Phone: (703) 528-0700
Fax: (703) 841-1543
http://www.aasa.org

American Cancer Society
1599 Clifton Rd., NE
Atlanta, GA 30329
Phone: (800) 227-2345
Fax: (404) 248-1780
http://www.cancer.org

American College of Sports Medicine
401 W. Michigan St.
Indianapolis, IN 46202-3233
Phone: (317) 637-9200
Fax: (317) 634-7817
http://www.acsm.org

American Dietetic Association
216 W. Jackson Blvd., Suite 800
Chicago, IL 60606
Phone: (312) 899-0040
Fax: (312) 899-1758
http://www.eatright.org

American Federation of Teachers
555 New Jersey Ave., NW
Washington, DC 20001
Phone: (202) 879-4490
Fax: (202) 393-8648
http://www.aft.org

American Medical Association
514 N. State St.
Chicago, IL 60610
Phone: (312) 464-5000
Fax: (312) 464-5842
http://www.ama-assn.org

American Nurses Association
600 Maryland Ave., SW
Suite 100 West
Washington, DC 20024
Phone: (800) 274-4262
Fax: (202) 651-7001
http://www.ana.org

American Psychological Association
750 First St., NE
Washington, DC 20002
Phone: (800) 374-2721
Fax: (202) 336-5962
http://www.apa.org

American Public Health Association
800 I St., NW
Washington, DC 20001-3710
Phone: (202) 777-2742
Fax: (202) 777-2534
http://www.apha.org

American Public Human Services Association
810 First St., NE, Suite 500
Washington, DC 20002
Phone: (202) 682-0100
Fax: (202) 289-6555
http://www.aphsa.org

American Red Cross
8111 Gatehouse Rd.
Jefferson Park
Falls Church, VA 22042
Phone: (703) 206-7180
Fax: (703) 206-7673
http://www.redcross.org

American School Counselor Association
801 N. Fairfax St., Suite 310
Alexandria, VA 22314
Phone: (703) 683-2722
Fax: (703) 683-1619
http://www.schoolcounselor.org

American School Food Service Association
700 South Washington St., Suite 300
Alexandria, VA 22314
Phone: (703) 739-3900
Fax: (703) 739-3915
http://www.asfsa.org

American School Health Association
PO Box 708
Kent, OH 44240
Phone: (330) 678-1601
Fax: (330) 678-4526
http://www.ashaweb.org

Association for Supervision & Curriculum Development
1703 North Beauregard St.
Alexandria, VA 22311-1714
Phone: (703) 578-9600
Fax: (703) 575-5400
http://www.ascd.org

Association of Maternal & Child Health Programs
1220 19 St., NW, Suite 801
Washington, DC 20036
Phone: (202) 775-0436
Fax: (202) 775-0061
http://www.amchp.org

Association of State & Territorial Chronic Disease Program Directors
111 Park Place
Falls Church, VA 22046-4513
Phone: (703) 538-1798
Fax: (703) 241-5603
http://www.astcdpd.org

Association of State & Territorial Dental Directors
322 Cannondale Rd.
Jefferson City, MO 65109
Phone: (573) 636-0453
Fax: (573) 636-0454
http://www.astdd.org

Association of State & Territorial Directors of Health Promotion and Public Health Education
750 First St., NE, Suite 1050
Washington, DC 20002
Phone: (202) 312-6460
Fax: (202) 336-6012
http://www.astdhpphe.org

Association of State & Territorial Health Officials
1275 K St., NW, Suite 800
Washington, DC 20005
Phone: (202) 371-9090
Fax: (202) 371-9797
http://www.astho.org

Association of State & Territorial Public Health Nutrition Directors
1015 15 St., NW, Suite 800
Washington, DC 20005
Phone: (202) 408-1257
Fax: (202) 408-1259
http://www.astphnd.org

California Department of Education
Safe and Healthy Kids Program Office
1430 N. Street, Suite 6408
Sacramento, CA 95814
Phone: (916) 319-0920
Fax: (916) 319-0218
http://www.cde.ca.gov/healthykids

California Healthy Kids Resource Center
313 W. Winton Ave., Room 180
Hayward, CA 94544
Phone: (510) 670-4581
Fax: (510) 670-4582
http://www.hkresources.org

Center for School Mental Health Assistance
University of Maryland-Baltimore,
Department of Psychiatry
680 W. Lexington St., 10th Floor
Baltimore, MD 21201-1570
Phone: (410) 706-0980
Fax: (410) 706-0984
http://www.csmha.umaryland.edu/
csmha2001/main.php3

Centers for Disease Control and Prevention (CDC)
1600 Clifton Rd., NE
Atlanta, GA 30333
Phone: (404) 639-3311
http://www.CDC.gov

Communities in Schools, Inc.
227 S. Washington St., Suite 210
Alexandria, VA 22314
Phone: (703) 519-8999
Fax: (703) 519-7213
http://www.clsnet.org

The Council for Exceptional Children
1110 N. Glebe Rd., Suite 300
Arlington, VA 22201-5704
Phone: (703) 620-3660
Fax: (703) 264-9494
http://www.cec.sped.org

Council of Chief State School Officers
One Massachusetts Ave., NW
Suite 700
Washington, DC 20001
Phone: (202) 408-5505
Fax: (202) 408-8072
http://www.ccsso.org

Council of the Great City Schools
1301 Pennsylvania Ave., NW
Suite 702
Washington, DC 20004
Phone: (202) 393-2427
Fax: (202) 393-2400
http://www.cgcs.org

Employee Assistance Professionals Association
2102 Wilson Blvd., Suite 500
Arlington, VA 22201
Phone: (703) 387-1000
Fax: (703) 522-4585
http://www.eap-association.org

Food Research and Action Center
1875 Connecticut Ave., NW,
Suite 540
Washington, DC 20009
Phone: (202) 986-2200
Fax: (202) 986-2525
http://www.frac.org

National Alliance for the Mentally Ill
Colonial Place Three
2107 Wilson Blvd., Suite 300
Arlington, VA 22201
Phone: (703) 524-7600
Fax: (703) 524-9094
http://www.nami.org

National Alliance of Pupil Services Organizations
7700 Willowbrook Rd.
Fairfax Station, VA 22039
Phone: (703) 250-3414
Fax: (703) 250-6324
https://www.socialworkers.org/

National Assembly on School-Based Health Care
666 11th St., NW, Suite 735
Washington, DC 20001
Phone: (888) 286-8727
Fax: (202) 638-5879
http://www.nasbhc.org

National Association for Sport and Physical Education
1900 Association Dr.
Reston, VA 20191-1599
Phone: (703) 476-3410
Fax: (703) 476-8316
http://www.aahperd.org/naspe/naspemain.html

National Association of Community Health Centers
1330 New Hampshire Ave., NW
Suite 122
Washington, DC 20036
Phone: (202) 659-8008
Fax: (202) 659-8519
http://www.nachc.org

National Association of County & City Health Officials
1100 17th St., NW, 2nd Floor
Washington, DC 20036
Phone: (202) 783-5550
Fax: (202) 783-1583
http://www.naccho.org

National Association of Elementary School Principals
1615 Duke St.
Alexandria, VA 22314
Phone: (703) 684-3345
Fax: (703) 518-6281
http://www.naesp.org

National Association of Health & Fitness
201 S. Capitol Ave., Suite 560
Indianapolis, IN 46225
Phone: (317) 237-5630
Fax: (317) 237-5632
http://www.physicalfitness.org

National Association of Leadership for Student Assistance Programs
PO Box 335
Bedminster, PA 18910
Phone: (215) 795-2119
Fax: (215) 795-0822

National Association of School Nurses
PO Box 1300
Scarborough, ME 04074-1300
Phone: (207) 883-2117
Fax: (207) 883-2683
http://www.nasn.org

National Association of School Psychologists
4340 East West Hwy., Suite 402
Bethesda, MD 20814
Phone: (301) 657-0270
Fax: (301) 657-0275
http://www.nasponline.org

National Association of Social Workers
750 First St., NE, Suite 700
Washington, DC 20002-4241
Phone: (202) 408-8600
Fax: (202) 336-8310
http://www.naswdc.org

National Association of State Boards of Education
277 S. Washington St., Suite 100
Alexandria, VA 22314
Phone: (703) 684-4000
Fax: (703) 836-2313
http://www.nasbe.org

National Association of State NET Program Coordinators
200 W. Baltimore St.
Baltimore, MD 21201
Phone: (410) 767-0222
Fax: (410) 333-2635

National Coalition for Parent Involvement in Education
3929 Old Lee Hwy., Suite 91-A
Fairfax, VA 22030-2401
Phone: (703) 359-8973
Fax: (703) 359-0972
http://www.ncpie.org

National Coalition of Chapter 1 and Title 1 Parents
Edmonds Schools Building
9th and D Sts., NE, Room 201
Washington, DC 20002
Phone: (202) 547-9286
Fax: (202) 547-2813
http://www.nctic1p.org/

National Conference of State Legislatures
1560 Broadway, Suite 700
Denver, CO 80202
Phone: (303) 830-2200
Fax: (303) 863-8003
http://www.ncsl.org

National Council of Churches
475 Riverside Dr.
New York, NY 10115
Phone: (212) 870-2297
Fax: (212) 870-2030
http://www.ncccusa.org

National Council of LaRaza
1111 19th St., NW, Suite 1000
Washington, DC 20036
Phone: (202) 785-1670
Fax: (202) 776-1792
http://www.nclr.org

National Education Association
1201 16th St., NW
Washington, DC 20036
Phone: (202) 883-4000
Fax: (202) 822-7775
http://www.nea.org

National Environmental Health Association
720 South Colorado Blvd., Suite 970-S
Denver, CO 80246
Phone: (303) 756-9090
Fax: (303) 691-9490
http://www.neha.org

National Federation of State High School Associations
PO Box 690
Indianapolis, IN 46206
Phone: (317) 972-6900
Fax: (317) 822-5700
http://www.nfhs.org

National Middle School Association
4151 Executive Parkway, Suite 300
Westerville, OH 43081
Phone: (800) 528-6672
Fax: (614) 895-4750
http://www.nmsa.org

National Network for Youth
1319 F St., NW, Suite 401
Washington, DC 20004
Phone: (202) 783-7949
Fax: (202) 783-7955
http://www.nn4youth.org

National Peer Helpers Association
PO Box 2684
Greenville, NC 27834
Phone: (877) 314-7337
Fax: (919) 522-3959
http://www.peerhelping.org

The National PTA
330 N. Wabash Ave., Suite 2100
Chicago, IL 60611-3690
Phone: (312) 670-6782
Fax: (312) 670-6783
http://www.pta.org

National Safety Council
1121 Spring Lake Dr.
Itasca, IL 60143-3201
Phone: (630) 285-1121
Fax: (630) 285-1315
http://www.nsc.org

National School Boards Association
1680 Duke St.
Alexandria, VA 22314
Phone: (703) 838-6722
Fax: (703) 683-7590
http://www.nsba.org

National Urban League
120 Wall St., 8th Floor
New York, NY 10005
Phone: (212) 558-5300
Fax: (212) 344-5332
http://www.nul.org

National Wellness Association
PO Box 827
Stevens Point, WI 54481-0827
Phone: (715) 342-2969
Fax: (715) 342-2979
http://www.nationalwellness.org

President's Council for Physical Fitness and Sports
Hubert H. Humphrey Building
200 Independence Ave., SW, Room 738H
Washington, DC 20201
Phone: (202) 690-9000
Fax: (202) 690-5211
http://www.fitness.gov

Public Education Network
601 13th St., NW, Suite 900 North
Washington, DC 20005
Phone: (202) 628-7460
Fax: (202) 628-1893
http://www.publiceducation.org

Public Risk Management Association
1815 N. Fort Meyer Dr., Suite 102
Arlington, VA 22209
Phone: (703) 528-7701
Fax: (703) 528-7966
http://www.primacentral.org

Society for Adolescent Medicine
1916 Copper Oaks Circle
Blue Springs, MO 64015
Phone: (816) 224-8010
Fax: (816) 224-8009
http://www.adolescenthealth.org

Society for Nutrition Education
1001 Connecticut Ave., NW, Suite 528
Washington, DC 20036-5528
Phone: (202) 452-8534
Fax: (202) 452-8536
http://www.sne.org

Society for Public Health Education, Inc.
750 First St., NE, Suite 910
Washington, DC 20002-4242
Phone: (202) 408-9804
Fax: (202) 408-9815
http://www.sophe.org

Society of State Directors of Health, Physical Education, and Recreation
1900 Association Dr.
Reston, VA 21091-1599
Phone: (703) 476-3402
Fax: (703) 476-9527
http://www.thesociety.org

State Directors of Child Nutrition
C/O AFSA
700 S. Washington St., Suite 300
Alexandria, VA 22314
Phone: (703) 739-3900
Fax: (703) 739-3915
http://www.asfsa.org

Wellness Councils of America
9802 Nicholas St., Suite 315
Omaha, NE 68114
Phone: (402) 827-3590
Fax: (402) 827-3594
http://www.welcoa.org

Diseases and Disorders: Background, Symptoms, and Classroom Implications

The following information about various communicable and noncommunicable diseases and disorders is provided for your reference. Background information, signs/symptoms, and school or classroom implications are given for each disease. Consult your school nurse or another medical authority if you have any questions or concerns about the health of your students.

Communicable Diseases and Disorders	Noncommunicable Diseases and Disorders
Chicken Pox (Varicella)	Anorexia Nervosa
Colds	Anthrax
Conjunctivitis (Pinkeye)	Appendicitis
Fifth Disease	Asthma
Hepatitis (Viral)	Bronchitis (Asthmatic or Allergic)
Human Immunodeficiency Virus (HIV) Infection and Acquired Immunodeficiency Syndrome (AIDS)	Cerebral Palsy (CP)
	Diabetes
	Down Syndrome
Impetigo	Epilepsy (Seizure Disorder)
Influenza	Hearing Loss
Measles (Rubella, or German Measles)	Heart Disorders
Measles (Rubeola)	Hemophilia (Bleeding Disorder)
Mononucleosis (Mono)	Leukemia
Mumps	Lyme Disease
Pediculosis (Lice)	Muscular Dystrophy
Ringworm (Tinea)	Peptic Ulcer
Scabies	Reye's Syndrome
Smallpox	Rheumatic Fever
Staphylococcal Infections (Staph)	Rheumatoid Arthritis
Strep Throat	Scoliosis
Sudden Acute Respiratory Syndrome (SARS)	Sickle-Cell Anemia
	Sty
Tonsillitis	Tendonitis
Tuberculosis (TB)	Tetanus (Lockjaw)
	Vision Disorders
	West Nile Virus

Communicable Diseases and Disorders

Infectious conditions, whether communicable among humans or noncommunicable, are receiving more medical and media attention. While much conversation is about agents that might be adapted to hurt or threaten groups, e.g., inhalation anthrax or smallpox, there is much more occurring with "emerging" and re-emerging infections. Several factors are involved: global work that exposes people to new infectious agents; intercontinental travel of people and transportation of animals that harbor infection or objects and insects that can transmit disease (vectors); population increases and crowding; public health and laboratory tests that can identify new organisms and give more specific reasons for illnesses; disrupted habitats (irrigation, deforestation) that allow organisms to jump to another species of animal; contaminated water as breeding ground for organisms; food preparation and distribution across the world; lagging vaccination rates; unrecognized "old" contagious conditions like whooping cough and tuberculosis; microbe resistance to drugs and pesticides; and fewer public health resources for malaria.

Chicken Pox (Varicella)

Background: Chicken pox (varicella) is caused by the varicella zoster virus. This virus can become dormant in nerve cells and later re-activate as shingles. Chicken pox is a relatively mild disease in children without other chronic conditions. However, Reye's syndrome, which can have serious results, is often preceded by salicylate (aspirin) use in viral illnesses such as chicken pox (see "Reye's syndrome" under "Noncommunicable Diseases and Disorders"). A vaccine is available for children between ages 12 and 18 months or older children who have not had varicella.

Symptoms: mild headache and moderate fever, a rash progressing to itching fluid-filled blisters, which then scab and crust over

Classroom Implications: Chicken pox is highly contagious and is spread by direct contact with blister fluid and through nasal discharge. Students may return to school when all the blisters have crusted over. Some may have complications such as pneumonia or secondary skin infection which delay their return.

Colds

Background: Colds are caused by viruses. More than a hundred such viruses have been found to produce the inflammatory reactions associated with colds. Therefore, colds can occur as many as four or five times a year. The key factor is exposure to an infected person. Being chilled does not cause a cold but may lower resistance to developing the disease after exposure.

Symptoms: a tickling sensation in the nose and throat, bouts of sneezing, watery nasal discharge, dulled senses of taste and smell, body aches, a cough, slight fever

Classroom Implications: Because cold and influenza viruses are highly infectious, a child with a "blossoming" cold (fever, cough, sneezes) should probably not be in school. However, many students attend school while recovering. Reinforcing hygiene with students, such as washing the hands regularly and covering the mouth with disposable tissue when coughing or sneezing, may limit the spread. Remember that a student with a fever/cold does not function at his or her best.

Conjunctivitis (Pinkeye)

Background: Conjunctivitis can be caused by viruses, bacteria, or allergies. Conjunctivitis is an inflammation of the membrane that covers the cornea or sclera (the white of the eye). Usually the condition is self-limiting. Viral pinkeye is contagious but there is no anti-viral treatment.

Symptoms: pink or red sclera, possibly discharge or crust on the eyelids, itching

Classroom Implications: Viral conjunctivitis is more contagious than bacterial. A student suspected of having pinkeye should be referred to the school nurse. Students should keep their hands clean, not share eye makeup (older girls), and not share face cloths with anyone who has pinkeye.

Fifth Disease

Background: Fifth disease is a mild illness caused by a virus (human parvovirus B19) usually during elementary school age years. If a woman gets the disease during pregnancy, it can infect the unborn child and, in rare cases, cause complications or death to the fetus. The virus is most likely spread by direct contact with saliva or nasal discharge.

Symptoms: begins with signs of a cold but develops a light red "lacy" rash that tends to come and go on the face, the trunk, and the arms and legs. In adults, joint swelling and pain can also occur.

Classroom Implications: Fifth disease is contagious before the rash appears, so it is often not diagnosed until children are no longer contagious. Children are not usually out of school unless running a fever. A pregnant teacher should discuss exposure with her doctor.

Hepatitis (Viral)

Background: Hepatitis is inflammation of the liver. Different viruses are known to cause some cases of viral hepatitis. They are named hepatitis A, B, C, D, and E viruses. All of them cause short-term, viral hepatitis. Hepatitis B, C, and D viruses can also cause chronic hepatitis, in which the infection is sometimes lifelong. Hepatitis A and E are spread through fecal contamination of water and food. Hepatitis B is spread through blood and certain body secretions, such as by sexual activity, blood exposure during childbirth, and the sharing of used needles for tattoos or drug use. Hepatitis C, the most common form, is spread by infected blood, less often by sexual activity or childbirth. Vaccines are available for hepatitis A and hepatitis B. Hepatitis D can occur in persons with hepatitis B.

Symptoms: nausea, vomiting, fever, loss of appetite during the early phase; jaundice, characterized by dark urine and light-color stools (feces) followed by yellowing of the body surfaces and the whites of the eyes (after three to ten days). Young children may have no signs of illness.

Classroom Implications: Though viral hepatitis resolves within weeks, it is a serious illness. General school exposure does not merit immune globulin. If more than one student in a class contracts hepatitis A, it may be prudent to ask about immune globulin for close contacts in the class. These injections provide some short-term protection against the virus. Good personal hygiene, such as washing hands carefully after changing diapers or helping younger children in the toilet, prevents the spread of the disease and should be emphasized. A student who misses school because of hepatitis will likely require home teaching until recovery is complete.

Human Immunodeficiency Virus (HIV) Infection and Acquired Immunodeficiency Syndrome (AIDS)

Background: HIV is the virus that causes AIDS. Most people with HIV infection develop AIDS.

The virus attacks the body's immune system, and infected people become susceptible to a variety of diseases that are usually not serious threats to people with normal immune systems. The AIDS diagnosis is determined by the presence of these infections and by blood tests. HIV is transmitted through contact with specific body fluids, including blood, semen, and vaginal secretions. It is not spread through the air, water, food, eating utensils, tears, sweat, or skin-to-skin contact. Early diagnosis and new drug treatments may interfere with the virus replication and reduce the risk of developing life-threatening infections.

Symptoms: nonspecific symptoms such as swollen lymph glands, loss of appetite, chronic diarrhea, weight loss, fever and fatigue; secondary viral and bacterial infections and cancers such as Kaposi's sarcoma

Classroom Implications: Most people can avoid exposure to HIV by avoiding risky behaviors such as unprotected sex and the sharing of needles. District health services policy should include guidelines to prevent exposure to body secretions, e.g., access to latex or vinyl gloves when assisting in first aid or direct health care.

Impetigo

Background: Impetigo is a skin infection seen mostly in children. It is usually caused by strains of strepto-coccal or staphylococcal bacteria. The infection usually appears on the fingers or face and is treated with antibiotics.

Symptoms: small blisters with pus; itchy, weeping sores that develop yellow, honey-colored crusts

Classroom Implications: Impetigo may be spread by direct contact. Students who have unexplained sores should be referred to the school nurse. Untreated lesions may cause scarring. Secondary infections in other parts of the body are possible. Students should be reminded to wash their hands and keep their fingernails clean. Sores should be lightly covered while under treatment to limit scratching or exposure to others.

Influenza

Background: The most frequent cause is the influenza A virus. It is spread by person-to-person contact and by droplets that become airborne because of coughing, sneezing, or talking. Major epidemics occur about every three years and affect persons of all ages. Influenza is most prevalent in school children. The very young, the aged, and persons with a chronic condition such as asthma, sickle-cell anemia, or diabetes are at the greatest risk of developing complications. Each year a vaccine is formulated to protect against the flu viruses expected to circulate the following winter. Those at greatest risk of complications from the virus should be among the first to receive the vaccine.

Symptoms: chills, fever, body aches and pains, headache, sore throat, cough, fatigue

Classroom Implications: Influenza is a self-limiting disease, with acute illness lasting for two to three days. Weakness and fatigue may persist for several days or occasionally for weeks. When a student returns to class after a bout with influenza, he or she may temporarily lack the ability to concentrate.

Measles (Rubella, or German Measles)

Background: Rubella is caused by a virus and is spread through personal contact and through airborne droplets. Rubella is milder and less contagious than rubeola, another type of measles. However, a pregnant woman who contracts rubella in early pregnancy risks serious injury to the fetus.

Symptoms: a rash that eventually covers the body, lasting about three days; mild fever; tenderness and swelling of the lymph nodes at the back of the neck

Classroom Implications: Prevention of rubella is a health priority because of the high risk during pregnancy. Children may be vaccinated between 12 and 15 months of age with a combination measles-mumps-rubella (MMR) vaccine and given a booster after age 4 years.

Measles (Rubeola)

Background: Rubeola is caused by a virus that is spread by nose, throat, and mouth droplets. It is most contagious two to four days before the rash begins and during the acute phase. Children should be vaccinated against rubeola. The recommended age for inoculation is between 12 and 15 months with a booster after age 4 years or by age 12 years if not done previously. The combined measles-mumps-rubella (MMR) vaccine is used.

Symptoms: high fever followed by hacking cough, sneezing, runny nose, redness of the eyes, sensitivity to light, a rash beginning at the face and moving down

Classroom Implications: About 20 percent of measles cases develop complications such as ear infections, pneumonia, or even encephalitis with lasting effects. All rubeola cases should be reported to the health authorities.

Infectious Mononucleosis (Mono)

Background: Infectious mononucleosis is caused by the Epstein-Barr virus, which is one of the herpes group of viruses. Mono is often called the "kissing disease," because it is spread by close contact with infected saliva. Mono is not very contagious. It may be positively diagnosed by a blood test.

Symptoms: fatigue, headache, chills, followed by high fever, sore throat, swelling of the lymph nodes. Enlargement of the spleen occurs in some.

Classroom Implications: Infection with the Epstein-Barr virus occurs commonly in children but often goes unrecognized, as it resembles a bad cold. Infectious mononucleosis, as described above, is predominantly more serious for adolescents and young adults. Symptoms can last weeks, and a variety of complications can occur. Many students with mono are out of school a long time and may be easily fatigued when allowed to return, which should be taken into consideration.

Mumps

Background: Mumps is caused by a virus that is spread by droplet infection or by materials that have been in contact with infected saliva. The virus predominantly affects the parotid salivary glands, which are located in the cheek area, in front of the ears. When infected, these glands swell, giving the person a chipmunk-like appearance. Occasionally, the salivary glands under the tongue become involved, and the neck area may swell.

Symptoms: chills, headache, loss of appetite, fever, pain when chewing or swallowing

Classroom Implications: Children may be vaccinated against mumps between ages 12 and 15 months with a booster after age 4 years (before entering school). The vaccine is usually given in a combined form with the measles and rubella vaccines. All mumps cases should be reported to the proper health authorities.

Pediculosis (Lice)

Background: Lice are small parasitic insects. Three types of lice are known to live on a human host. Crab lice *(Phthirus pubis)* are usually transmitted by very close contact, such as during sex or sharing a bed or towel. Body lice *(Pediculus humanus corporis)* are uncommon under good hygienic conditions. Head lice *(Pediculus humanus capitis)* are transmitted by personal contact: by contact with an infested person (contact is common during play at school and at home at slumber parties, during sports activities, at camp, or on a playground); by wearing infested clothing, such as hats, scarves, coats, sports helmets, or hair ribbons; by using infested combs, brushes, or towels; by lying on a bed, couch, pillow, carpet, or stuffed animal that has recently been in contact with an infested person.

Head lice invade the scalp but can also move to the eyebrows, eyelashes, and other facial hair. The lice lay eggs, called nits, which are grayish white and can be seen adhering to the hair shafts. The nits mature in three to fourteen days.

Symptoms: itching, white nits (eggs) that tightly adhere to the hair shafts

Classroom Implications: Teachers should reinforce prevention habits and limit "head-to-head" group work as well as observe for possible signs, e.g., scratching. If a student in class has lice, other students should be discreetly checked with a hand lens by a person trained to identify lice and nits. The lice can be killed with specially medicated shampoo or creams. Parents/caretakers should be advised to remove the nits to prevent re-infestation. Students should be welcomed back in the classroom following effective treatment.

Ringworm (Tinea)

Background: Ringworm is an infection caused by any of a number of fungi that invade only the dead tissue (keratin) of skin, hair or nails. Infection by a certain fungus can produce raised rings on the skin (hence the name *ringworm*). However, other fungi cause different signs. The various fungi attack specific areas of the body.

Symptoms: slowly spreading, scaly, ring-shaped spots on the skin (ringworm of the body, *tinea corporis*); scaling lesions between the toes ("athlete's foot," *tinea pedis*); thickened, lusterless nails with a darkened appearance (ringworm of the nails, *tinea unguium*); small, scaly lesions on the scalp and semibald, grayish patches with broken, lusterless hairs (ringworm of the scalp, *tinea capitis*)

Classroom Implications: The most common types of ringworm are "athlete's foot" and ringworm of the scalp. Athlete's foot is often spread at swimming pools and in showers, locker rooms, and other such wet facilities. Ringworm of the scalp mainly affects children. If this condition is suspected, a student should immediately be referred to the school nurse. Scalp ringworm requires oral prescribed medication to penetrate the hair follicles.

Scabies

Background: Scabies is an infectious parasitic skin infection caused by the itch mite *(Sarcoptes scabiei)*. Pregnant female mites tunnel into the skin and deposit their eggs. The larvae hatch after a few days and group around the hair follicles. Itching is due to hypersensitivity to the parasites' waste products. Scabies is transmitted through prolonged, not casual, skin-to-skin contact, often infecting entire households. It can be spread through shared clothing or bedding.

Symptoms: intense itching; burrows (fine, wavy, dark lines with small pimple-like lesions at the open ends) occurring commonly between the fingers; burrows also occurring on the insides of the wrists and in skin folds on the abdomen and elbows

Classroom Implications: Suspected scabies needs to be referred to health professionals and treated immediately. Prescribed lotions are necessary and the student may also have medication to relieve itching, which can last a month after treatment while dead skin and mites are shed.

Smallpox

Background: Smallpox is a highly contagious disease that was eliminated in the world in 1977. Vaccination was no longer indicated and the vaccine can have serious side effects. There is some concern that the smallpox virus could be used as a weapon of bioterrorism. There is a smallpox preparedness program to protect Americans against smallpox as a biological weapon. This program includes training teams to respond to a smallpox attack. Healthcare and public health workers are being vaccinated in order to care for and vaccinate others in the event of an outbreak. There is enough smallpox vaccine to vaccinate everyone who would need it.

Symptoms: The incubation period for smallpox is from 7 to 17 days following contact with the virus. Symptoms include high fever, fatigue, headache, and backache. A rash follows in 2 to 3 days. The rash begins as a flat red spot that becomes filled with pus and then begins to crust early in the second week. Scabs form and then fall off after 3 to 4 weeks.

Classroom Implications: Smallpox is spread from person to person by infected droplets of saliva. Persons are most contagious during the first week of illness but may be contagious during the entire period of illness. There is no cure for smallpox, but if the vaccine is given within 4 days of exposure to the virus, it can lessen the severity of the illness or even prevent it.

Staphylococcal Infections (Staph)

Background: Staphylococcal bacteria are commonly found on the skin of healthy people. Those who are hospitalized or work in hospitals have a slightly higher incidence of penicillin-resistant strains. Staph food poisoning is caused by the toxin produced by the staphylococci in contaminated food.

Symptoms: General: fever, headache; Skin: boils, abscesses, skin lesions with pus (impetigo); Food: vomiting

Classroom Implications: All staph infections should be treated promptly by a health professional. Suspect food poisoning when a number of people develop vomiting within hours of eating a food in common, often involving improperly prepared or stored products. Report names, symptoms and food(s) eaten, because staph is just one of the possible culprits.

Strep Throat

Background: Strep throat is caused by one form of streptococcal bacterium. A throat culture can confirm the presence of streptococcal bacteria.

Symptoms: sudden fever and headache, sore, beefy-red throat, nausea or vomiting, swollen neck "glands"; inflamed tonsils with thin white patches on tonsils. Cases that include a rash that is due to a toxin produced by the strep bacteria are called scarletina or scarlet fever.

Classroom Implications: Complications of strep throat can be life-threatening. Rheumatic fever with joint or heart disease or a kidney complication may develop in a small percentage of cases. Therefore, it is very important that students who show symptoms of the disease be evaluated. Any student with fever and sore throat without a cough, laryngitis, or stuffy nose should be suspect.

Sudden Acute Respiratory Syndrome (SARS)

Background: This unusual pneumonia is believed to be caused by a virus in the coronavirus family that exists in wild animals used for food in China. With laboratory advances, the cause of SARS was determined within three months of the early cases—great progress compared to the four years it took to identify HIV.

Symptoms: After 2 to 7 (up to 10) days from exposure, an ill person has fever (over 100°), headache, muscle aches, dry cough, and difficulty breathing.

Classroom Implications: With travel restrictions, young students are unlikely to be exposed. Travelers, family, or health workers exposed to infected persons must stay home for a 10-day "health watch" to monitor for symptoms. Infection control includes standard precautions (hand washing) and air precautions (surgical mask for the patient, air filtration in hospitals) with patients with symptoms and exposure. This is a topic that can be used to encourage students to apply the "disease detective" work of epidemiology to an array of health conditions.

Tonsillitis

Background: Tonsillitis is an acute inflammation of the tonsils, often caused by viruses or common bacteria.

Symptoms: sore throat and pain, especially upon swallowing; fever, headache, vomiting, white patches on the tonsils

Classroom Implications: Repeated tonsillitis may cause frequent absences pending medical evaluation. When students return to school after tonsillectomies, there are usually few restrictions on their activity.

Tuberculosis (TB)

Background: Tuberculosis is an acute or chronic disease caused by a rod-shaped bacterium. TB is primarily a pulmonary disease but can strike other organs and tissues, such as bones. Infection usually occurs after exposure from inhaling infectious droplets. The bacteria settle in the lower or middle section of the lungs and multiply. The body's immune system then fights the disease, producing antibodies against it. Infection may continue to be contained without disease developing. The bacteria may reactivate in persons with lowered resistance due to other chronic conditions. TB exposure is detected by the tuberculin skin test (PPD), and disease is determined by lab tests and a chest X–ray.

Symptoms: fever, body aches, chronic cough that expels sputum

Classroom Implications: In the United States TB has reemerged as a serious public health problem, affecting low income groups that live in close quarters and persons who do not get tested or who do not complete treatment. Drug-resistant cases of TB have also increased dramatically because of incomplete treatment. TB is primarily an airborne disease. Children do not cough deeply enough to spread TB bacteria if they have an infection. Public health officials hire staff to ensure that some infected persons complete their antibiotic treatment to avoid more drug-resistance and spread to others.

© Harcourt

Noncommunicable Diseases and Disorders

Anorexia Nervosa

Background: Anorexia nervosa is a psychological condition, an eating disorder that is usually most common among adolescent girls. The disease is characterized by a distorted concept of body image and involves extreme weight loss. Many people with the disorder look emaciated but are convinced they are overweight. Bulimia nervosa is a variant of anorexia nervosa. It is characterized by eating binges followed by purges. Purging may involve vomiting, abusing laxatives or diuretics, taking enemas, exercising obsessively, or a combination of these. As body fat decreases, the menstrual cycle is interrupted.

Symptoms: rapid weight loss, change in eating habits, obsession with exercise to lose weight, increased use of laxatives, depressed mental state, cessation of menstruation, sores around the mouth and dental disease from forced vomiting

Classroom Implications: Eating disorders such as anorexia nervosa and bulimia nervosa may occur in varying severity. They are more successfully treated when diagnosed early. Many cases have been discovered by teachers who have made appropriate referrals. Students with eating disorders need the emotional support of their teachers. Efforts to enhance realistic body image and self-concept in the classroom contribute toward treatment goals.

Anthrax

Background: Anthrax is a noncommunicable infectious disease usually found in cloven-hoofed animals. It can also infect humans. Anthrax infection takes one of three possible forms. They are inhalation, cutaneous, and gastrointestinal. Inhalation anthrax involves inhaling *Bacillus anthracis*. This is the most serious form of infection. Cutaneous, or skin infection, involves transmission through a cut or rash on the skin. This is the least serious form of infection but has been around for centuries. Gastrointestinal infection occurs when infected meat is ingested. Between January 1955 and December 1999, there were 236 reported cases of anthrax in the United States. Most of those cases were cutaneous and occurred among persons who worked with contaminated animal products. Anthrax has been used as an agent of bioterrorism within the United States. A vaccine is available for the prevention of anthrax infection. Antibiotic treatment is available for persons who have been exposed to anthrax or who have developed the disease.

Symptoms: Inhalation: sore throat, mild fever, muscle aches, and general malaise. Respiratory failure, shock, and meningitis often occur.

Cutaneous: a small pimple that enlarges to an ulcer that is black in the center. Fever, headache, malaise, and swollen lymph nodes can be present.

Gastrointestinal: This results from eating raw or undercooked contaminated meat. There is severe abdominal distress with fever and severe diarrhea.

Classroom Implications: Because anthrax cannot be transmitted from person to person, there is little likelihood that there will be an outbreak in the classroom. However, with anthrax being an agent of bioterrorism, be vigilant with unknown substances that may come from unusual sources. Don't open any packages or mail that may be suspicious. Contact the appropriate authorities if you suspect anthrax contamination.

Appendicitis

Background: Appendicitis is most common in adolescents and young adults but is also a major reason for abdominal surgery in children. The appendix becomes infected with bacteria normally found in the bowel. Continued inflammation may lead to abscess formation, gangrene, and perforation resulting in peritonitis.

Symptoms: steady, localized pain, usually in the lower right abdominal quadrant; constipation that began recently; nausea and vomiting; mild fever; elevated white-blood-cell count

Classroom Implications: A student returning to the classroom after an appendectomy may have restrictions on his or her activity for a time. The student may tire easily the first few days and have difficulty concentrating.

Asthma

Background: Asthma is a chronic reversible airway condition that results in recurring attacks of breathing problems. Attacks can be triggered by upper respiratory infections (colds or flu); hard exercise; laughing or crying hard; allergies to common substances such as animal dander (tiny scales from skin), pollen, or dust; irritants such as cold air, strong smells, and chemical sprays (perfume, paint and cleaning solutions, chalk dust, lawn and turf treatments); weather changes; or tobacco smoke. During an attack the muscles surrounding the bronchial tubes tighten, thus reducing the size of the airway. The allergic response causes mucus production and a resultant productive cough. People with asthma are able to draw air into the lungs through the narrowed airway but are unable to expel carbon dioxide waste out. They may cough, wheeze, gasp for air, and feel that they are suffocating.

Symptoms: wheezing, gasping for air, hacking cough, tightness in the chest, shortness of breath

Classroom Implications: An asthma attack may be compared to taking a deep breath and not being able to let it out. A student having an asthma attack should be reassured that help is on the way. People with asthma are often fearful of the attacks. An attack may occur at any time and may be triggered by emotional strain, physical exertion, or environmental factors. Many students with asthma take prescription prevention (control) and rescue (acute) medicines, which should be available to them when needed. These medicines may cause jitteriness, overactivity, or, rarely, drowsiness. With medical management and monitoring with peak flow meters at home and school, students with asthma usually have few restrictions on activity, except during or following an acute attack.

Bronchitis (Asthmatic or Allergic)

Background: Bronchitis is inflammation of the bronchial tubes. It may develop as a result of an environmental irritant like cigarette smoke or from an upper-respiratory infection. A virus or bacterium invades the area and causes inflammation and increases mucus secretion. A deep, rumbling cough develops. Treatment is directed at drainage and expulsion of the mucus rather than at suppression of the cough.

Symptoms: chills, slight fever, back and muscle pain, sore throat, followed by dry cough and then by a cough that expels mucus

Classroom Implications: Bronchitis is a self-limiting disease in most cases; complete healing usually occurs within a few weeks. The student who has bronchitis, however, may be absent and may require help in making up missed work.

Cerebral Palsy (CP)

Background: Cerebral palsy is a term for a group of non-progressive motor disorders that impair voluntary movement. The various forms of CP are caused by developmental problems or injury to the motor areas of the central nervous system before, during, or soon after birth. Physical therapy helps many people with CP overcome their disabilities.

Symptoms: spasticity of limbs, weakness, limb deformities, speech disorders, involuntary movements, difficulty with fine movements, visual disturbances; commonly accompanied by nerve deafness, mental impairment, or seizure disorders

Classroom Implications: Students with severe CP can be mainstreamed with therapy services and support. In mild forms of CP, the symptoms may be seen only during certain activities, such as running. Students with mild CP have the usual range of intelligence and function in a regular classroom setting. Be aware of the student's particular needs, and include the student in classroom activities. Discussing the disorder with classmates and explaining why the student may sometimes move differently will increase understanding and help eliminate teasing. Drugs can be used to control seizures and muscle spasms; special braces can compensate for muscle imbalance. Surgery and mechanical aids can help to overcome impairments. Counseling and physical, occupational, speech, and behavioral therapy may be included in the student's education plan.

Diabetes

Background: Diabetes is characterized by an increase of sugar (glucose) in the blood, which also spills into the urine. In type 1 diabetes, an autoimmune disorder, cell groups in the islets of Langerhans of the pancreas no longer secrete adequate amounts of the hormone insulin. Insulin is the primary substance that allows the body to utilize sugar. In type 2 diabetes, there is a genetic predisposition to develop diabetes along with significant overweight and low physical activity that interferes with the body's use of available insulin to move sugar into the body cells, especially the muscle and fat tissue cells. There is no known cure but research is exploring pancreas cell transplantation for type 1. Optimal treatment usually consists of regulated insulin replacement (by injection or pump), self-monitoring of blood glucose, daily diet, and exercise.

Symptoms: fatigue, frequent urination, thirst, hunger, weight loss (type 1), infections that do not heal quickly

Classroom Implications: Teachers are often in a position to help identify undiagnosed diabetes. Any changes in bathroom or drinking habits should be investigated. Unexplained weight loss or the inability to concentrate or new irritability should also be suspect. A student with regulated diabetes functions normally in the classroom. If you have a student requiring insulin shots, keep a source of sugar, such as orange juice, available for low insulin (hypoglycemia) episodes. You need to accommodate a student on insulin or oral medications for type 2 diabetes who must have a snack once or twice a day at school, self-check blood glucose non-disruptively in the classroom, self-inject insulin on schedule or as the monitoring results indicate. Physical education and meal/snack time need to be coordinated.

Down Syndrome*

Background: Down syndrome is an inherited condition that is usually associated with an extra chromosome. Fifty percent of infants with the syndrome are born to mothers over the age of 35.

Genetic conditions named for individuals are spelled without 's, as recommended by the American Society of Human Genetics.

© Harcourt

Children with Down syndrome have a mean IQ of 50. They usually have small heads and slanted eyes. Life expectancy is normal in the absence of other birth defects, such as heart disease.

Symptoms: placidity, poor muscle tone; slanted eyes, flattened nosebridge; mouth usually held open because of enlarged tongue; short-fingered, broad hands with single crease; feet with a wide gap between the first and second toes

Classroom Implications: Children with Down syndrome often have special education resources to meet their individual needs and group activities such as Special Olympics. But many students are part of the regular classroom community. Their classmates need to understand conditions that make others different. A careful introduction to disabilities is a must for the whole class.

Epilepsy (Seizure Disorder)

Background: Epilepsy, a disorder of the nerve cells in the brain, is characterized by episodes of muscle spasms or strange sensations called seizures. The well-known kinds of generalized seizures are grand mal, petit mal, and psychomotor or temporal lobe. During a seizure, brain impulses become chaotic, causing the person to lose full consciousness and control over body movement.

Symptoms: uncontrollable jerking movements followed by a deep sleep (tonic-clonic seizure or convulsion); momentary cessation of movement (absence seizure); coordinated but strange whole body movements while in altered consciousness (simple partial or complex partial seizure)

Classroom Implications: If a student is known to have seizures, get details about the specific type, medications, and what to expect. In a tonic-clonic seizure, do not attempt to restrain the person. If the student has not fallen, gently move him or her onto the floor and move any obstructions out of the way. Do not place any objects in the student's mouth. A convulsive seizure may be a frightening experience to witness, so offer others a simple explanation and reassurance. Absence seizures, though less dramatic, make the student unresponsive with rapid blinking or other behavior; the student briefly loses consciousness. Anticonvulsive medications have side effects, such as drowsiness or making concentration difficult. Computer screens, video games, and flashing lights have been known to trigger seizures. People with epilepsy follow safety guidelines such as wearing helmets for bike riding or climbing, and swimming only with a life jacket at all times.

Hearing Loss

Background: Many conditions can produce hearing loss. Conduction deafness can be caused by sound waves being blocked by wax or by scars from middle-ear infections. It can also be caused by Eustachian tube dysfunction, middle ear fluid, or fixation of the bones of the middle ear. Most of these conditions can be reversed, and normal hearing can be restored. However, when the auditory nerve is damaged, such as by disease or prolonged loud noise, little can be done.

Symptoms: apparent inattention, frequent asking for repetition of what was said, frequent misunderstanding of verbal directions, failure to respond to normal voices or sounds, cupping of the ear to funnel sounds

Classroom Implications: Students with diagnosed hearing loss may require special seating and aids in the classroom. Some students need to wear one or two hearing aids, which should be explained to the rest of the class. Other amplification aids should be supplied when needed. If you observe changes in any student's ability to hear, make referrals for testing.

Heart Disorders

Background: Many conditions can cause heart disorders. The most common disorders in infancy and early childhood are congenital abnormalities such as valve problems, holes between right and left chambers (septal defects), and failure of an opening between the aorta and the pulmonary artery to close after birth (a condition called patent ductus arteriosus). These conditions can be surgically corrected in most instances. Another type of heart condition is a heart murmur, a series of prolonged heart sounds that can be heard as vibrations. Some murmurs are significant but most are not; they are called functional and usually disappear in time. Some significant murmurs may signal developmental heart-valve abnormalities.

Symptoms: shortness of breath, chest pain, blue tinge to the skin, fatigue, slowing of heartbeat rate, palpitations

Classroom Implications: Children who have had surgical correction for congenital heart disorders usually lead restriction-free lives. Those who have continuing problems or who develop additional problems may have to curtail physical activity, and you may need to make special plans for them. All students should be encouraged to develop good physical fitness habits and healthful eating habits to help reduce the risk for adult causes of heart disease such as high cholesterol.

Hemophilia (Bleeding Disorder)

Background: Hemophilia is one inherited bleeding disorder. Others include von Willebrand and platelet disorders. The person is unable to manufacture certain essential clotting factors and therefore might bleed to death or suffer joint damage if a cut or bruise is left untreated.

Symptoms: serious bleeding or bruising from minor injuries or normally lost tooth or heavy menstrual period

Classroom Implications: Most students who have bleeding disorders can lead normal lives if they are receiving treatment for the missing blood clotting factor. However, you should be aware of this condition and take necessary precautions to prevent injury. First-aid procedures for external and internal bleeding should be reviewed with the school nurse or with a physician. Minor episodes may be treated with a prescribed nasal spray medication.

Leukemia

Background: Leukemia is a cancer of white blood cells that eventually crowd out normal white, red, and platelet blood cells. There are several types of leukemia. Acute lymphoblastic leukemia (ALL) primarily affects children. Acute myeloid leukemia (AML) can occur in people of any age. In all people with leukemia, abnormal white blood cells form in large numbers. In children, the causes are unclear and may include genetic tendencies and conditions such as Down syndrome.

Symptoms: high fever and joint pain; bleeding from the mouth, nose, kidneys, and large intestine; enlarged liver, spleen, and lymph nodes

Classroom Implications: Continual improvement in chemotherapy has made remissions (absences of any signs of the disease) much more common, especially in acute lymphoblastic leukemia. Students undergoing treatment for leukemia may be able to return to school after the acute stage of the disease has been arrested. However, depending on the treatment schedule, they may have to return to the hospital periodically. Every effort to maintain continuity in the classroom for these students should be made. Many of the drugs that are administered cause hair loss, which should be explained to the rest of the class. Sometimes students become frightened by the word cancer, and questions such as "Can I catch it?" "Will he die?" and "Will I die?" may be asked. Dealing with these types of concerns openly and honestly may alleviate fear and anxiety.

Lyme Disease

Background: Lyme disease is caused by a spirochete that is transmitted to humans by deer ticks.

Symptoms: After 3 to 32 days from a tick bite exposure (lasting 12 or more hours), a skin lesion begins as a red spot or bump, but enlarges to look like a "bull's eye." Other signs are flu-like tiredness, chills, muscle and joint pain, and swollen lymph glands. Complications include joint arthritis, Bell's palsy, and heart rate irregularities.

Classroom Implications: Persons conducting school outings in areas infested by ticks should instruct students to wear protective clothing and to check hourly for ticks. Any ticks should be removed with an appropriate technique and the site cleaned.

Muscular Dystrophy

Background: The muscular dystrophies are a group of inherited progressive diseases that produce a breakdown in the muscle fibers, causing increasing weakness and difficulty with movement and breathing. Duchenne muscular dystrophy is the most common form. It occurs in boys 3 to 7 years of age. The disease causes a steady increase in muscle weakness, and most patients use a wheelchair by the age of 10 or 12.

Symptoms: muscle weakness causing a waddling gait, toe-walking, a swaybacked appearance, frequent falls, difficulty in standing up and in climbing stairs

Classroom Implications: Many children with muscular dystrophy, especially the less common, milder forms, are mainstreamed. If one of your students has muscular dystrophy, you need to be aware of his or her specific progression and limitations. Special equipment along with physical and occupational therapy may be needed for instruction and for support. Fostering understanding among classmates is of utmost importance.

Peptic Ulcer

Background: A peptic (stomach) ulcer is a sore or hole in the stomach or the first part of the small intestine (duodenum). It used to be thought that a peptic ulcer was a chronic disease that resulted from the overproduction of gastric juices manufactured by the stomach to break down foods. However, in the mid-1980s it was discovered that most ulcers may be caused by a bacterium, *Helicobacter pylori*. These ulcers can be cured with antibiotics. The course of treatment lasts for two weeks and can permanently cure the ulcer. Peptic ulcers are relatively common among adults, though they do occur in children, even before the age of 10.

Symptoms: a painful burning sensation, usually relieved by meals and occurring at night; nausea and vomiting if the pain is severe; constipation; anemia

Classroom Implications: Students who complain of persistent, localized stomach pain should see a physician. Most often a course of antibiotics will be prescribed.

Reye's Syndrome

Background: The cause of Reye's syndrome is currently unknown. Reye's syndrome (RS) is primarily a children's disease, although it can occur at any age. It affects all organs of the body but is most harmful to the brain and the liver—causing an acute increase of pressure within the brain and, often, massive accumulations of fat in the liver and other organs. The disorder commonly occurs during recovery from a viral infection, although it can also develop 3 to 5 days after the onset of the viral illness (most commonly influenza or chicken pox). The cause of RS remains a mystery. However, studies have shown that using aspirin or salicylate-containing medications to treat viral illnesses increases the risk of developing RS.

Symptoms: uncontrollable nausea and vomiting about the sixth day after a viral infection; noticeable change in mental function; lethargy, mild amnesia, disorientation, agitation, unresponsiveness, coma, seizures, fixed and dilated pupils

Classroom Implications: Parents should be informed of the possible link between aspirin and Reye's syndrome. Some people recover completely, while others may sustain varying degrees of brain damage. The syndrome may leave permanent neurological damage, causing mental retardation or problems with movement.

Rheumatic Fever

Background: Rheumatic fever is a possible secondary complication of a streptococcal infection, especially strep throat. Rheumatic fever is an acute inflammatory reaction to the streptococcal bacterium and can affect one or more major sites, including the joints, the brain, the heart, and the skin. The disease is rare before 4 years of age and uncommon after age 18.

Symptoms: varied symptoms appearing alone or in combination after a severe sore throat: a flat, painless rash, lasting less than a day; painless nodules on the legs; swollen tender joints; recurrent fevers; movement disorders.

Classroom Implications: Since rheumatic fever can develop to varying degrees, the amount of physical restriction depends on the joint and cardiac problems of the individual. Psychological problems have been noted in students who have been restricted from play because they have rheumatic fever. It is important for all parents and school personnel to see that a student with a possible strep infection is treated promptly. Any changes in a student's work habits, appearance, or energy level after a strep infection should be investigated.

Rheumatoid Arthritis

Background: Rheumatoid arthritis is a chronic autoimmune disorder characterized by inflammation of the joints. The immune system, for unknown reasons, attacks a person's own cells inside the joint capsule. White blood cells travel to the synovium and cause a reaction. As rheumatoid arthritis progresses, these abnormal synovial cells destroy the cartilage and bone within the joint. The surrounding muscles, ligaments, and tendons that support and stabilize the joint become weak.

In children the knees, elbows, wrists, and other large joints tend to be affected. This may result in interference with growth and development. In some cases the eyes and heart are affected. Complete remission is more likely in children than in adults.

Symptoms: rash, fever, inflammation of the irises, enlargement of the spleen and lymph nodes; swelling, pain, and tenderness of the involved joints

Classroom Implications: A student with rheumatoid arthritis may be absent frequently because of the chronic, recurring nature of the disease and may need help in keeping up with schoolwork. Stiffness of joints and possible deformities may limit the student's movement. Restrictions on the student's activity can be less burdensome if you explain the situation to the whole class. Emotional support from classmates can contribute to the student's sense of well being. Care usually includes healthy lifestyle (diet, exercise, and rest), stress management, medications for pain and inflammation, and sometimes joint surgery.

Scoliosis

Background: Scoliosis is a lateral curvature of the spine. This disorder occurs most commonly during the adolescent growth period. It is estimated that between 5 and 10 percent of school age children have a single or double spinal curvature in varying degrees. However, only about 2 percent of the cases are significant. The effect of scoliosis depends on its severity, how early it is detected, and treatment adherence. The curve usually does not get worse once the spine has reached full growth. Scoliosis is more common among girls than boys.

Symptoms: unequal shoulder levels, a hunchbacked appearance (kyphosis or C-shaped curve), fatigue or muscle aches in the lower back region, persistent back pain

Classroom Implications: Many states now require scoliosis screening for preadolescent and adolescent students. Treatment of scoliosis may range from monitoring to muscle development exercises, to bracing, or to corrective surgery. Special braces or casts can threaten a teenager's self-concept. Therefore, counseling and support from teachers, parents, and peers are very important in treating a youngster with scoliosis.

Sickle-Cell Anemia

Background: Sickle-cell anemia is an inherited disease that affects African Americans mainly but not exclusively. Anemias are conditions in which the blood is low in red blood cells or in hemoglobin, causing a decrease in the body's ability to transport oxygen to all cells. This disease is named after the abnormal, sickle shape of some red blood cells that was a protective adaptation to fight malaria. Because of their shape these cells are not able to flow easily through the capillaries and tend to jam up around joints and in organs. This inhibiting of blood flow can cause acute pain.

Symptoms: fatigue, painful crises when blood vessels are blocked, yellow skin and eyes (jaundice), enlarged spleen, poor growth and delayed puberty, vision abnormalities

Classroom Implications: Sickle-cell anemia can cause repeated painful crisis situations that may require hospital treatment. A student with the disease may be out of school frequently and will need help in completing schoolwork and maintaining contact with the class. Support students' self-care which includes drinking extra water, pain medicines at school, moderate exercise, diet rich in folic acid, avoiding extreme cold and heat, and avoiding exposure to infections.

Sty

Background: Sties are inflamed hair follicles or glands on the eyelids. They are usually caused by staphylococcal bacteria.

Symptoms: a tiny abcess on the eyelid, redness, tenderness of the eyelid, sensitivity to light, the feeling of having a foreign body in the eye

Classroom Implications: Students who develop sties should be referred to the school nurse and may improve with the application of warm compresses. If not improved in 2–3 days, referral to a physician is indicated. Sties are not contagious.

Tendonitis

Background: Tendonitis is an inflammation of the tendons surrounding various joints (shoulder, elbow, wrist, and knee most often). The inflammation usually results from a joint being forced beyond its normal range of motion or in an abnormal direction. Excessive exercise or repeated injury to a joint may also cause tendonitis. A common form of tendonitis, tennis elbow, results from the excessive rotation of the forearm and hand while playing tennis. The muscles of the forearm are strained, and the inflammation spreads to the elbow.

Symptoms: swelling, local tenderness, disabling pain when the affected joint is moved

Classroom Implications: Students may develop tendonitis from excessive periods of repeated exercise such as pitching a baseball or hitting a tennis ball. Students who spend many hours working the levers of video games may experience tendonitis of the wrist joint. Tendonitis may often be prevented through proper coaching in technique and appropriate periods of rest. Cross-training mixes impact-loading exercise, such as running, with lower-impact exercise, such as biking or swimming. Students who complain of constant, disabling pain in any joint should be referred for medical evaluation.

Tetanus (Lockjaw)

Background: Tetanus is an acute infectious disease caused by a bacterium that produces spores and that can live in an environment without oxygen, namely soil or animal feces. Once the toxin from the bacterium enters the body, it interferes with the central nervous system's ability to transmit impulses

correctly. This causes a generalized spasticity and intermittent convulsive movements. Stiffness of the jaw is a classic symptom of tetanus (hence the name lockjaw). The typical route of transmission is through a skin wound, usually a dirty splinter or puncture wound, such as from a knife or nail that has been contaminated with dirt containing the spores. The spores then develop into bacteria that release the toxin. Primary immunization against tetanus begins in infancy with a booster at school age. This is given in the form of a DTaP (diphtheria-tetanus-acellular pertussis) combination vaccine. After that, booster injections should be administered every 10 years lifelong.

Symptoms: stiff jaw muscles and difficulty in swallowing; restlessness and irritability; stiffness in the neck, arms, or legs; headache, fever, sore throat, chills, convulsions

Classroom Implications: Help students clean all wounds promptly and thoroughly to prevent exposure. If a student suffers a deep wound and has not had a tetanus booster within five years, his/her doctor may order a booster within two days. Following first aid, all wounds of concern should be reported to the school nurse for proper evaluation.

Vision Disorders

Background: There are three common eye disorders that produce errors in refraction and that decrease visual acuity. The most common childhood disorder is farsightedness (hyperopia), which interferes with the ability to see clearly things that are nearby. In nearsightedness (myopia) a person is able to see things clearly that are near, but distance vision is impaired. Astigmatism, or distorted vision, occurs when there are defective curvatures of the refractive surfaces of the cornea. Other conditions such as eye muscle imbalance also interfere with clear binocular vision. Young children may suppress poorer vision in one eye and, if not treated, in preschool years may permanently lose the vision in that eye (developing amblyopia).

Symptoms: head tilt, squinting, headaches, eye muscle fatigue, holding reading material unusually close or far away, complaining of not being able to see the board, inability to do fine motor or sport tasks as well as expected for age and overall development.

Classroom Implications: Make sure vision screening and any referrals are completed as soon as possible to limit the risk of amblyopia. Students with undiagnosed eye disorders may have a difficult time with schoolwork. As a teacher you are in an excellent position to note such problems and to make appropriate referrals. Reinforce wearing and care for glasses as prescribed, and refer families that need community resources to get needed glasses (not usually covered by health insurance).

West Nile Virus

Background: The West Nile virus (WNV) was first known in 1937 and is in the family Flavivirus, related to the type that causes St. Louis encephalitis. WNV arrived in the US about 1999 through imported animals and objects. Generally, WNV is spread by the bite of an infected mosquito. Mosquitoes harbor the virus in the salivary glands after feeding on infected birds. Infected mosquitoes can then spread WNV to humans and other animals they bite.

Symptoms: WNV affects the central nervous system. Most people (80 percent) will not show any symptoms. Up to 20 percent will have mild symptoms for a few days, including fever, headache, body aches, nausea, vomiting, and sometimes swollen lymph glands or a skin rash (trunk). About one in 150

people infected with WNV will develop severe illness: high fever, headache, neck stiffness, coma, tremors, convulsions, muscle weakness, vision loss, numbness, and paralysis. These symptoms may last several weeks, and neurological effects may be permanent.

Implications: The best way to avoid WNV is to prevent mosquito bites. School buildings should have good screens on windows and doors. Get rid of mosquito breeding sites by emptying standing water. Drill drainage holes in tire swings so water drains out. Keep children's wading pools empty and on their sides when not being used. During activities, precautions should be taken. When outdoors, use insect repellents containing DEET (N, N-diethyl-meta-toluamide). Wear long sleeves and pants.

© Harcourt

Name _____   Date _____

School-Home Connection

What We Are Learning About Health

In Chapter 1 of *Harcourt Health and Fitness,* we are learning about

- the interdependence, structure, and function of body organs, and how they work together as systems.
- the physical and emotional changes that accompany adolescence and the importance of lifelong health habits.
- communicating to family members regarding changing wants and needs.
- respecting everyone regardless or how he or she differs from others.

 Visit **www.harcourtschool.com/health** for links to parent resources.

How You Can Help

Parental involvement in the school environment is part of a coordinated school health plan that includes the home, school, community, and social services. You can support your school through increased communication and by volunteering your time or talents. At home you can support your child's learning by

- discussing the changes you went through during puberty and adolescence.

- encouraging your child to talk about any concerns he or she may have about getting older.

- discussing the similarities and differences of people in your own neighborhood.

A Family Activity

As people grow, they pass through several stages. Talk with your child about major events that have affected his or her development during two stages—infancy and childhood. Work together to record these events in the following table. For the sections entitled "Adolescence" and "Adulthood," help your child anticipate some of the major events that he or she may experience during these stages, such as graduation from high school or full-time employment.

Stages of Growth

	Events in Your Life
Infancy	
Childhood	
Adolescence	
Adulthood	

La escuela y la casa

Nota para los familiares

Lo que estamos aprendiendo acerca de la Salud

En el Capítulo 1 de *Harcourt Health and Fitness* estamos aprendiendo acerca de:

- La interdependencia, estructura y función de los órganos del cuerpo y cómo trabajan como sistemas.
- Los cambios físicos y emocionales que acompañan a la adolescencia y la importancia de tener hábitos saludables de por vida.
- Cómo comunicarse con los miembros de la familia acerca de deseos y necesidades cambiantes.
- El respeto que se le debe tener a todas las personas aunque sean diferentes.

 Visite **www.harcourtschool.com/health** para encontrar enlaces con recursos en inglés para los padres.

Cómo puede usted ayudar

La participación familiar en las actividades escolares forma parte de un plan de salud organizado que incluye la casa, la escuela, la comunidad y los servicios sociales. Usted puede apoyar a la escuela manteniendo una buena comunicación y ofreciendo su tiempo y sus talentos como voluntario. En casa, usted puede apoyar el aprendizaje de su hijo(a) haciendo lo siguiente:

- Hablen acerca de los cambios que usted sufrió durante la pubertad y la adolescencia.
- Anime a su hijo(a) a que hable de cualquier preocupación que tenga sobre su crecimeinto.
- Hablen acerca de las semejanzas y las diferencias de las personas que viven en su barrio.

Actividad familiar

Las personas, al crecer, pasan por diferentes etapas. Hable con su hijo(a) acerca de los sucesos más importantes que han afectado su desarrollo durante dos etapas: la primera y la segunda infancia. Trabajen juntos para documentar estos sucesos en la tabla siguiente. Para las secciones tituladas "Adolescencia" y "Edad adulta", ayude a su hijo(a) a anticipar algunos de los sucesos más importantes que es posible que experimente durante estas etapas, tales como la graduación del bachillerato o el obtener un empleo de tiempo completo.

Etapas del crecimiento

	Sucesos importantes en su vida
Primera infancia	
Segunda infancia	
Adolescencia	
Edad adulta	

© Harcourt

Name _____ Date _____

School-Home Connection

What We Are Learning About Health

In Chapter 2 of *Harcourt Health and Fitness,* we are learning about

- the importance of good hygiene, including taking care of skin, hair, and nails.
- using technology wisely and safely.
- making responsible decisions when choosing health-care products.
- demonstrating fairness by not taking advantage of others, by looking out for their interests, and by being honest.

Visit **www.harcourtschool.com/health** for links to parent resources.

How You Can Help

Parental involvement in the school environment is part of a coordinated school health plan that includes the home, school, community, and social services. You can support your school through increased communication and by volunteering your time or talents. At home you can support your child's learning by

- discussing your own personal hygiene habits.
- examining how you can both use technology better.
- praising your child's fairness and honesty when dealing with others.

A Family Activity

Good hygiene is an important part of being healthy. What can children do to make sure they have good hygiene? Ask your child to fill in the table below. When the table is finished, discuss how your family can support good personal hygiene.

Good Hygiene Habits

Body Part	What I Do to Take Care of It
Skin	
Teeth	
Eyes	
Ears	
Gums	

© Harcourt

La escuela y la casa

Nota para los familiares

Lo que estamos aprendiendo acerca de la Salud

En el Capítulo 2 de *Harcourt Health and Fitness* estamos aprendiendo acerca de:

- La importancia de una higiene adecuada, incluyendo el cuidado de la piel, el cabello y las uñas.
- Cómo usar la tecnología con sabiduría y seguridad.
- Cómo tomar decisiones responsables al elegir productos para el cuidado de la salud.
- Cómo demostrar justicia, al no aprovecharse de otros, cuidar de sus intereses y ser honestos.

 Visite **www.harcourtschool.com/health** para encontrar enlaces con recursos en inglés para los padres.

Cómo puede usted ayudar

La participación familiar en las actividades escolares forma parte de un plan de salud organizado que incluye la casa, la escuela, la comunidad y los servicios sociales. Usted puede apoyar a la escuela manteniendo una buena comunicación y ofreciendo su tiempo y sus talentos como voluntario. En casa, usted puede apoyar el aprendizaje de su hijo(a) haciendo lo siguiente:

- Hablen acerca de los hábitos de higiene personal que usted tiene.
- Examinen cómo pueden usar la tecnología de una manera mejor.
- Elogie su sentido de justicia y su honestidad en su trato con los demás.

Actividad familiar

El tener una higiene adecuada es muy importante para estar sanos. ¿Qué pueden hacer los niños para asegurarse de tener buenos hábitos de higiene personal? Pida a su hijo(a) que llene la siguiente tabla. Cuando la complete, hablen acerca de cómo su familia puede ayudar a propiciar buenos hábitos de higiene personal.

Buenos hábitos de higiene personal

Parte del cuerpo	Qué cuidado le doy
Piel	
Dientes	
Ojos	
Oídos	
Encías	

School-Home Connection

A Note to Family Members

What We Are Learning About Health

In Chapter 3 of *Harcourt Health and Fitness,* we are learning about

- the six basic nutrients and how they work together to help keep the body healthy.
- foods from around the world and their nutritional benefits.
- reading food labels when shopping, and asking the correct questions about food when eating out.
- practicing self-control when choosing a snack.

 Visit **www.harcourtschool.com/health** for links to parent resources.

How You Can Help

Parental involvement in the school environment is part of a coordinated school health plan that includes the home, school, community, and social services. You can support your school through increased communication and by volunteering your time or talents. At home you can support your child's learning by

- examining different foods from around the world.

- practicing how to read food product labels in your home.

- praising your child for choosing a healthful snack over one that is not.

A Family Activity

This chapter offers some opportunities for adding spice and variety to your family's weekly menu while ensuring that your family eats a well-balanced diet. With your child, prepare and serve one of the recipes presented in the chapter—Chicken Soft Tacos (page 90), Stir-Fried Tofu and Vegetables (page 93), or Beef Kabobs (page 95). Your child can then ask one or two family members to rate the dish.

Recipe: _____

Family Member	Comments

© Harcourt

La escuela y la casa

Nota para los familiares

Lo que estamos aprendiendo acerca de la Salud

En el Capítulo 3 de *Harcourt Health and Fitness* estamos aprendiendo acerca de:

• Los seis nutrientes básicos y cómo trabajan juntos para ayudar a mantener sanos nuestros cuerpos.

• Los alimentos de diferentes partes del mundo y sus beneficios nutricionales.

• Cómo leer las etiquetas de los alimentos cuando van de compras y cómo hacer preguntas adecuadas acerca de la comida cuando comen fuera.

• Cómo practicar el autocontrol al elegir refrigerios.

 Visite **www.harcourtschool.com/health** para encontrar enlaces con recursos en inglés para los padres.

Cómo puede usted ayudar

La participación familiar en las actividades escolares forma parte de un plan de salud organizado que incluye la casa, la escuela, la comunidad y los servicios sociales. Usted puede apoyar a la escuela manteniendo una buena comunicación y ofreciendo su tiempo y sus talentos como voluntario. En casa, usted puede apoyar el aprendizaje de su hijo(a) haciendo lo siguiente:

• Examinen alimentos de diferentes partes del mundo.

• Practiquen cómo leer las etiquetas de productos alimenticios que tengan en casa.

• Elogie a su hijo(a) por elegir un refrigerio saludable en lugar de uno que no lo es.

Actividad familiar

Este capítulo le ayuda a añadir novedad y variedad al menú semanal de la familia, al mismo tiempo que se asegura de que su familia tenga una dieta bien balanceada. Con su hijo(a), prepare y sirva una de las recetas que se presentan en este capítulo: Chicken Soft Tacos (Tacos suaves de pollo, página 90), Stir-Fried Tofu and Vegetables (Tofú y vegetales salteados, página 93) o Beef Kabobs (Brocheta de carne, página 95). Luego, su hijo(a) puede pedir a uno o dos familiares que den su opinión del platillo.

Receta:_____

Familiar	Comentarios

© Harcourt

Name _____ Date _____

School-Home Connection

A Note to
Family Members

What We Are Learning About Health

In Chapter 4 of *Harcourt Health and Fitness,* we are learning about

- becoming physically fit and maintaining a healthy weight through exercise.
- exercising with safety in mind by using self-discipline and safety equipment.
- setting up schedules for reaching fitness goals and improving fitness levels.
- being a good sport by following rules and playing fair.

 Visit **www.harcourtschool.com/health** for links to parent resources.

How You Can Help

Parental involvement in the school environment is part of a coordinated school health plan that includes the home, school, community, and social services. You can support your school through increased communication and by volunteering your time or talents. At home you can support your child's learning by

- stressing the importance of exercising throughout life.
- encouraging your child to use the proper safety equipment and procedures when exercising.
- studying the rules of your child's favorite game or sport.

A Family Activity

Many community organizations, such as hospitals, schools, YMCAs, and senior centers, offer low-cost physical fitness programs. Ask your child to find out about the programs available in your community. Help your child check a variety of advertising sources, such as local newspapers, supermarket bulletin boards, and phone books. Students can enter their findings in the following table and share the table with family members or neighborhood friends.

Fitness Programs in Your Community

Description of Activity	Where	When	Phone Number

Nombre _____ Fecha _____

La escuela y la casa

Lo que estamos aprendiendo acerca de la Salud

En el Capítulo 4 de *Harcourt Health and Fitness* estamos aprendiendo acerca de:

- Cómo lograr una buena condición física y mantener un peso adecuado por medio del ejercicio.
- Cómo hacer ejercicio de manera segura, con autodisciplina y un equipo de seguridad.
- Cómo establecer un horario adecuado para lograr metas de acondicionamiento físico y para mejorar los niveles de acondicionamiento.
- Cómo ser un buen participante en los deportes, al obedecer las reglas y jugar limpiamente.

Cómo puede usted ayudar

La participación familiar en las actividades escolares forma parte de un plan de salud organizado que incluye la casa, la escuela, la comunidad y los servicios sociales. Usted puede apoyar a la escuela manteniendo una buena comunicación y ofreciendo su tiempo y sus talentos como voluntario. En casa, usted puede apoyar el aprendizaje de su hijo(a) haciendo lo siguiente:

- Enfatice la importancia del ejercicio físico durante las diferentes etapas de la vida.
- Anímelo a usar equipo y procedimientos de seguridad adecuados al hacer ejercicios.
- Apréndase las reglas del juego o deporte favorito de su hijo(a).

 Visite **www.harcourtschool.com/health** para encontrar enlaces con recursos en inglés para los padres.

Actividad familiar

Muchas organizaciones de la comunidad, tales como los hospitales, las escuelas, los centros YMCA y los centros para personas de la tercera edad, a menudo ofrecen programas de acondicionamiento físico a bajo precio. Pida a su hijo(a) que investigue acerca de los programas que están disponibles en su comunidad. Ayúdelo a chequear varias fuentes de publicidad, tales como periódicos locales, tableros de supermercados y guías telefónicas. Cuando termine, puede registrar lo que encuentre en la siguiente tabla y mostrársela a sus familiares o amigos del barrio.

Programas de acondicionamiento físico en tu comunidad

Descripción de la actividad	Dónde	Cuándo	Número telefónico

School-Home Connection

A Note to Family Members

What We Are Learning About Health

In Chapter 5 of *Harcourt Health and Fitness,* we are learning about

- staying safe in the home from electricity, fire, poison, and hazards in the kitchen.
- safety outside the home, including bicycle and automobile safety, water safety, and staying safe from weapons.
- listening, negotiating, and compromising to resolve conflicts that could lead to violence.
- how rules keep games and sports fair and safe.

 Visit **www.harcourtschool.com/health** for links to parent resources.

How You Can Help

Parental involvement in the school environment is part of a coordinated school health plan that includes the home, school, community, and social services. You can support your school through increased communication and by volunteering your time or talents. At home you can support your child's learning by

- discussing ways to make your home a safer place.
- encouraging your child to come up with ways to stay safe outside.
- praising your child for resolving conflicts peacefully.

A Family Activity

It is important that your child be able to notify the proper authorities in case of emergency. Help your child to fill out the following emergency telephone list. Use your local telephone directory to obtain the correct phone numbers. Have your child make one or more copies to place near home phones. Tell family members where the lists are located.

Emergency Telephone Numbers

Police	
Fire	
Poison Control	
Ambulance	
Emergency	911 or 0 (zero)

La escuela y la casa

Nota para los familiares

Lo que estamos aprendiendo acerca de la Salud

En el Capítulo 5 de *Harcourt Health and Fitness* estamos aprendiendo acerca de:

- Cómo evitar accidentes en el hogar con electricidad, fuego, sustancias tóxicas y peligros en la cocina.
- Seguridad fuera del hogar, incluyendo seguridad en bicicletas, en automóviles, y en el agua, y cómo mantenerse alejado de todo tipo de armas.
- Escuchar, negociar y llegar a un acuerdo como una manera de resolver conflictos que puedan generar violencia.
- Cómo las reglas ayudan a que los juegos y deportes se realicen de una manera segura y justa.

Cómo puede usted ayudar

La participación familiar en las actividades escolares forma parte de un plan de salud organizado que incluye la casa, la escuela, la comunidad y los servicios sociales. Usted puede apoyar a la escuela manteniendo una buena comunicación y ofreciendo su tiempo y sus talentos como voluntario. En casa, usted puede apoyar el aprendizaje de su hijo(a) haciendo lo siguiente:

- Hablen acerca de lo que pueden hacer para que su hogar sea un lugar más seguro.
- Anímelo a pensar en medidas que puede tomar para mantenerse seguro(a) cuando está fuera de casa.
- Elógielo cuándo resuelva conflictos pacíficamente.

 Visite **www.harcourtschool.com/health** para encontrar enlaces con recursos en inglés para los padres.

Actividad familiar

Es importante que su hijo(a) sea capaz de notificar a las autoridades correspondientes en casos de emergencia. Ayúdelo a completar la tabla con los números telefónicos de emergencia. Usen su guía telefónica local para obtener los números correctos. Pídale que haga una o más copias de la tabla para colocarlas cerca de los teléfonos en casa. Digan a sus familiares dónde han colocado esas listas.

Números telefónicos de emergencia

Policía	
Bomberos	
Centro de control de envenenamientos	
Ambulancia	
Emergencias	911 o 0 (cero)

Name _____   Date _____

School-Home Connection

A Note to Family Members

What We Are Learning About Health

In Chapter 6 of *Harcourt Health and Fitness,* we are learning about

- preparing for and responding to emergency situations.
- first aid for common injuries and life-threatening situations.
- effective communication when dealing with an emergency.
- showing responsibility by following safety rules that protect both rescuers and victims.

 Visit **www.harcourtschool.com/health** for links to parent resources.

How You Can Help

Parental involvement in the school environment is part of a coordinated school health plan that includes the home, school, community, and social services. You can support your school through increased communication and by volunteering your time or talents. At home you can support your child's learning by

- putting together emergency supply and first aid kits.

- discussing times when you have had to use first aid.

- praising your child's effective communication efforts.

A Family Activity

There are many different situations that call for first aid inside and outside the home. After your child has reviewed this chapter, test his or her knowledge about first aid. Have your child fill out the table, and then discuss what kinds of situations might lead to the need for these techniques.

First Aid

Injury or Situation	What to Do
Broken bone or fracture	
Sprain	
Burn	
Seizure	
Hyperthermia	
Hypothermia	

La escuela y la casa

Lo que estamos aprendiendo acerca de la Salud

En el Capítulo 6 de *Harcourt Health and Fitness* estamos aprendiendo acerca de:

• Cómo prepararse y actuar en situaciones de emergencia.
• Primeros auxilios para heridas comunes y situaciones de vida o muerte.
• Cómo lograr una comunicación efectiva cuando hay una emergencia.
• Cómo mostrar responsabilidad al seguir reglas de seguridad que protegen tanto a los socorristas como a las víctimas.

 Visite **www.harcourtschool.com/health** para encontrar enlaces con recursos en inglés para los padres.

Cómo puede usted ayudar

La participación familiar en las actividades escolares forma parte de un plan de salud organizado que incluye la casa, la escuela, la comunidad y los servicios sociales. Usted puede apoyar a la escuela manteniendo una buena comunicación y ofreciendo su tiempo y sus talentos como voluntario. En casa, usted puede apoyar el aprendizaje de su hijo(a) haciendo lo siguiente:

• Reúnan artículos para formar un botiquín de primeros auxilios y un kit de provisiones de emergencia.
• Hablen acerca de las ocasiones en las que hayan usado primeros auxilios.
• Elógielo cuándo se esfuerza por mantener una comunicación efectiva.

Actividad familiar

Hay muchas situaciones, tanto dentro como fuera del hogar, que requieren de primeros auxilios. Después de que su hijo(a) haya repasado este capítulo, compruebe sus conocimientos acerca de los primeros auxilios. Pídale que complete la siguiente tabla y hablen acerca de las situaciones en las que pueda llegar a necesitar estas técnicas.

Primeros auxilios

Lesión o situación	Qué hacer
Fractura o rotura de hueso	
Torcedura	
Quemadura	
Convulsión	
Hipertermia	
Hipotermia	

School-Home Connection

A Note to
Family Members

What We Are Learning About Health

In Chapter 7 of *Harcourt Health and Fitness,* we are learning about

• communicable and noncommunicable diseases and how they are transmitted.

• living well to promote a healthy life through exercise, a balanced diet, and getting enough sleep.

• recognizing and managing unhealthful stress.

• showing concern and caring for someone who is ill.

 Visit **www.harcourtschool.com/health** for links to parent resources.

How You Can Help

Parental involvement in the school environment is part of a coordinated school health plan that includes the home, school, community, and social services. You can support your school through increased communication and by volunteering your time or talents. At home you can support your child's learning by

• discussing someone in your family who has dealt with having a disease.

• encouraging your child to come up with exercise that he or she enjoys.

• praising your child's efforts to comfort and help an ill family member.

A Family Activity

Organisms that cause communicable diseases are called pathogens. People frequently practice habits that spread pathogens. For example, people may share a glass of water or milk, or they may reuse silverware without washing it. Ask your child to make a list in the space provided of habits that family members can practice to avoid the spread of infectious diseases. Discuss ways in which family members can help each other implement these practices.

Healthful Habits to Prevent the Spread of Illness

La escuela y la casa

Nota para los familiares

Lo que estamos aprendiendo acerca de la Salud

En el Capítulo 7 de *Harcourt Health and Fitness* estamos aprendiendo acerca de:

- Las enfermedades contagiosas y no contagiosas y cómo se trasmiten.
- Cómo fomentar una vida sana por medio de buenos hábitos como el ejercicio físico, una dieta balanceada y el descanso adecuado.
- Cómo reconocer y controlar la tensión que puede llegar a ser nociva.
- Cómo mostrar nuestra preocupación y cuidar de un enfermo.

Cómo puede usted ayudar

La participación familiar en las actividades escolares forma parte de un plan de salud organizado que incluye la casa, la escuela, la comunidad y los servicios sociales. Usted puede apoyar a la escuela manteniendo una buena comunicación y ofreciendo su tiempo y sus talentos como voluntario. En casa, usted puede apoyar el aprendizaje de su hijo(a) haciendo lo siguiente:

- Hablen de alguien en su familia que haya sufrido alguna enfermedad.
- Anímelo a pensar en algún ejercicio físico que disfrute.
- Elógielo cuando vea que trata de confortar y ayudar a un familiar enfermo.

 Visite **www.harcourtschool.com/health** para encontrar enlaces con recursos en inglés para los padres.

Actividad familiar

Los organismos que causan enfermedades contagiosas se llaman patógenos. Las personas frecuentemente tienen hábitos que propagan patógenos. Por ejemplo, algunas personas toman del mismo vaso de agua o leche, o usan los mismos utensilios de mesa sin antes lavarlos. Pida a su hijo(a) que haga una lista de los hábitos que la familia puede practicar para evitar la propagación de enfermedades infecciosas. Hablen acerca de las maneras en que los familiares pueden ayudarse unos a otros a implementar estas prácticas.

Hábitos para prevenir la propagación de enfermedades

© Harcourt

Name _____ Date _____

School-Home Connection

A Note to Family Members

What We Are Learning About Health

In Chapter 8 of *Harcourt Health and Fitness,* we are learning about

- the safe use of medicines and how they can relieve pain and cure illnesses.
- the harmful effects of abusing medicines and of using illegal drugs.
- saying *no* to using illegal drugs.
- showing citizenship by following laws and listening to authorities.

 Visit **www.harcourtschool.com/health** for links to parent resources.

How You Can Help

Parental involvement in the school environment is part of a coordinated school health plan that includes the home, school, community, and social services. You can support your school through increased communication and by volunteering your time or talents. At home you can support your child's learning by

- explaining how medicines have helped you in the past.
- discussing the use of illegal drugs in your community.
- role-playing with your child refusing negative peer pressure.

A Family Activity

Prescription medicines are very strong drugs. Physicians order medicine for one person only. It is very important that only that person use the medicine and that the medicine be used only as directed. Show your child a container of prescription medicine, and point out the following information on the label: name of the person it was prescribed for, name and address of the pharmacy, name of the doctor who prescribed the medicine, expiration date of the medicine, dosage, directions for use, warnings and cautions, and refill information. Explain what this information means, and emphasize that your child should take a medicine only with adult supervision.

La escuela y la casa

Nota para los familiares

Lo que estamos aprendiendo acerca de la Salud

En el Capítulo 7 de *Harcourt Health and Fitness* estamos aprendiendo acerca de:

- El uso adecuado de los medicamentos y cómo pueden ayudar a aliviar el dolor y a curar las enfermedades.
- El efecto nocivo del uso inadecuado de medicamentos y del uso de drogas ilegales.
- Cómo negarse a usar drogas ilegales.
- Cómo demostrar que se es un buen ciudadano al obedecer las leyes y a las autoridades.

 Visite **www.harcourtschool.com/health** para encontrar enlaces con recursos en inglés para los padres.

Cómo puede usted ayudar

La participación familiar en las actividades escolares forma parte de un plan de salud organizado que incluye la casa, la escuela, la comunidad y los servicios sociales. Usted puede apoyar a la escuela manteniendo una buena comunicación y ofreciendo su tiempo y sus talentos como voluntario. En casa, usted puede apoyar el aprendizaje de su hijo(a) haciendo lo siguiente:

- Explíquele cómo los medicamentos lo han ayudado en el pasado.
- Hablen acerca del uso de drogas ilegales en su comunidad.
- Improvisen situaciones en las que su hijo(a) no se deje llevar por las influencias negativas de sus compañeros.

Actividad familiar

Los medicamentos alópatas son drogas muy poderosas. Los doctores recetan medicamentos para una persona determinada. Es muy importante que solo esa persona use esos medicamentos y que los tome de la forma indicada. Muestre a su hijo(a) un recipiente de algún medicamento alópata y dirija su atención a la siguiente información en la etiqueta: nombre de la persona a quien se le recetó y dirección de la farmacia, nombre del doctor que lo recetó, fecha de caducidad, dosis, instrucciones de uso, advertencias e información para el reabastecimiento. Explique qué significa esta información y enfatice que su hijo(a) solamente debe tomar medicamentos bajo la supervisión de un adulto.

© Harcourt

Name _____ Date _____

School-Home Connection

A Note to Family Members

What We Are Learning About Health

In Chapter 9 of *Harcourt Health and Fitness,* we are learning about

- the harmful effects of alcohol and tobacco on the body.
- situations that might lead people to use alcohol and tobacco.
- ways to refuse alcohol and tobacco.
- showing trustworthiness by being honest, telling the truth, and keeping promises.

 Visit **www.harcourtschool.com/health** for links to parent resources.

How You Can Help

Parental involvement in the school environment is part of a coordinated school health plan that includes the home, school, community, and social services. You can support your school through increased communication and by volunteering your time or talents. At home you can support your child's learning by

- praising your child's understanding of why not to use alcohol or tobacco.
- discussing the use of alcohol and tobacco in your community.
- practicing with your child ways to refuse alcohol and tobacco from peers.

A Family Activity

Ask your child to find out about local programs that provide young people with alternatives to drinking. Recreation centers, parks, and youth organizations frequently sponsor these programs. Ask your child to record his or her findings in the following table. Then discuss the table with your child. Work together to brainstorm other activities that could be made available.

Local Programs

Name of Program	Where	When	Phone Number

© Harcourt

La escuela y la casa

Nota para
los familiares

Lo que estamos aprendiendo acerca de la Salud

En el Capítulo 9 de *Harcourt Health and Fitness* estamos aprendiendo acerca de:

• Los efectos nocivos del alcohol y del tabaco en el cuerpo.
• Situaciones que pueden inducir a las personas al uso del alcohol y del tabaco.
• Maneras de rehusarse a usar alcohol y tabaco.
• Cómo mostrar que se es digno de confianza al actuar honestamente, decir la verdad y cumplir las promesas.

 Visite **www.harcourtschool.com/health** para encontrar enlaces con recursos en inglés para los padres.

Cómo puede usted ayudar

La participación familiar en las actividades escolares forma parte de un plan de salud organizado que incluye la casa, la escuela, la comunidad y los servicios sociales. Usted puede apoyar a la escuela manteniendo una buena comunicación y ofreciendo su tiempo y sus talentos como voluntario. En casa, usted puede apoyar el aprendizaje de su hijo(a) haciendo lo siguiente:

• Elógielo cuando comprenda por qué no debe usar alcohol o tabaco.
• Hablando acerca del uso del alcohol y tabaco en su comunidad.
• Practiquen maneras de rechazar el alcohol o tabaco que le ofrezcan sus compañeros.

Actividad familiar

Pida a su hijo(a) que investigue acerca de los programas locales que ofrecen a los jóvenes alternativas al uso del alcohol. Los centros de recreación, parques y organizaciones juveniles frecuentemente patrocinan estos programas. Pídale que anote lo que encuentre en la siguiente tabla. Luego hablen acerca de lo que escribió. Piensen en otras actividades que se podrían ofrecer.

Programas locales

Nombre del programa	Dónde	Cuándo	Número de teléfono

© Harcourt

School-Home Connection

What We Are Learning About Health

In Chapter 10 of *Harcourt Health and Fitness,* we are learning about

• the relationship between self-concept, setting goals, and self-respect.
• strategies that effectively help deal with anger, stress, grief, and other unpleasant feelings.
• managing stress at school, such as when having to give a speech in front of the class.
• being a dependable friend through trust and support.

 Visit **www.harcourtschool.com/health** for links to parent resources.

How You Can Help

Parental involvement in the school environment is part of a coordinated school health plan that includes the home, school, community, and social services. You can support your school through increased communication and by volunteering your time or talents. At home you can support your child's learning by

• encouraging your child to set goals that uphold his or her good self-concept.

• discussing different ways to deal with stress.

• talking about your own friendships over the years.

A Family Activity

As a family, discuss the challenges that newcomers often face in becoming part of a community. Have family members share memories of times in their lives when they had to adjust to new surroundings. Have each person talk about the people who helped him or her adjust and how they helped. Using the table below, work together to list the names of recent newcomers to your neighborhood, school, or community. Have each family member suggest a way he or she could help make a newcomer feel welcome.

Welcome to the Community!

Name of Newcomer	Ways to Make the Newcomer Feel Welcome

La escuela y la casa

Nota para los familiares

Lo que estamos aprendiendo acerca de la Salud

En el Capítulo 10 de *Harcourt Health and Fitness* estamos aprendiendo acerca de:

- La relación entre la autoimagen, las metas que se proponen y el respeto a sí mismos.
- Estrategias efectivas para resolver problemas que tengan que ver con la ira, el estrés, la tristeza y otros sentimientos desagradables.
- Cómo controlar el estrés en la escuela, por ejemplo: cuando se tiene que dar un discurso frente a la clase.
- Cómo ser un amigo confiable que brinda apoyo a los demás.

 Visite **www.harcourtschool.com/health** para encontrar enlaces con recursos en inglés para los padres.

Cómo puede usted ayudar

La participación familiar en las actividades escolares forma parte de un plan de salud organizado que incluye la casa, la escuela, la comunidad y los servicios sociales. Usted puede apoyar a la escuela manteniendo una buena comunicación y ofreciendo su tiempo y sus talentos como voluntario. En casa, usted puede apoyar el aprendizaje de su hijo(a) haciendo lo siguiente:

- Anímelo a establecer metas que reflejen su buena autoimagen.
- Hablen sobre las diferentes formas de controlar el estrés.
- Hablen acerca de las amistades que usted ha cultivado durante su vida.

Actividad familiar

En familia, hablen de los retos que los recién llegados a menudo enfrentan en una comunidad. Pidan a algunos familiares que hablen acerca de los momentos en su vida en que tuvieron que adaptarse a nuevos lugares y de las personas que los ayudaron a adaptarse. En la siguiente tabla, hagan una lista de las personas recién llegadas a su barrio, escuela o comunidad. Pidan a cada familiar que sugiera algo que puede hacer para que esa persona se sienta bienvenida.

¡Bienvenido a la comunidad!

Nombre del recién llegado	Qué hacer para que se sienta bienvenido

© Harcourt

School-Home Connection

A Note to Family Members

What We Are Learning About Health

In Chapter 11 of *Harcourt Health and Fitness*, we are learning about

- how responsibility and self-discipline are important parts of growing up and maintaining family structures.
- the essentials of cooperation and communication in a successful family.
- resolving conflicting needs and wants between family members.
- the importance of caring in a strong and healthy family.

 Visit **www.harcourtschool.com/health** for links to parent resources.

How You Can Help

Parental involvement in the school environment is part of a coordinated school health plan that includes the home, school, community, and social services. You can support your school through increased communication and by volunteering your time or talents. At home you can support your child's learning by

- discussing how you became more disciplined as you matured.
- encouraging your child to talk about any new wants and needs he or she has.
- praising your child for caring about and taking an interest in family matters.

A Family Activity

Have your child use the following questions to interview a middle-aged or elderly adult family member about that person's experiences during his or her teenage years. Discuss the responses with your child. How have families changed? How have families remained the same?

Family Interview Sheet

1. Describe your family when you were a teenager.

2. What were your responsibilities?

3. How did your responsibilities change as you got older?

4. What was your favorite family activity?

5. Did you have a different favorite family activity as you got older?

La escuela y la casa

Nota para los familiares

Lo que estamos aprendiendo acerca de la Salud

En el Capítulo 11 de *Harcourt Health and Fitness* estamos aprendiendo acerca de:

- Cómo el ser responsables y autodisciplinados es una parte importante del crecimiento y la estructura familiar.
- Cómo coopera y se comunica una familia que vive en armonía.
- Cómo satisfacer necesidades y deseos que causan conflictos entre miembros de la familia.
- La importancia de la bondad dentro de una familia unida y sana.

 Visite **www.harcourtschool.com/health** para encontrar enlaces con recursos en inglés para los padres.

Cómo puede usted ayudar

La participación familiar en las actividades escolares forma parte de un plan de salud organizado que incluye la casa, la escuela, la comunidad y los servicios sociales. Usted puede apoyar a la escuela manteniendo una buena comunicación y ofreciendo su tiempo y sus talentos como voluntario. En casa, usted puede apoyar el aprendizaje de su hijo(a) haciendo lo siguiente:

- Hablen acerca de cómo usted se volvió más disciplinado(a) cuando maduró.
- Anímelo a hablar de algún nuevo deseo o necesidad que tenga.
- Elógielo por su bondad y por su interés en los asuntos de la familia.

Actividad familiar

Pida a su hijo(a) que use las siguientes preguntas para entrevistar a un adulto o anciano de su familia acerca de sus experiencias durante la adolescencia. Hablen acerca de las respuestas. ¿En qué han cambiado las familias? ¿En qué han permanecido iguales?

Hoja de entrevistas a familiares

1. Describa a su familia cuando usted era un adolescente.

2. ¿Cuáles eran sus responsabilidades?

3. ¿Cómo cambiaron sus responsabilidades cuando creció?

4. ¿Cuál era su actividad familiar favorita?

5. ¿Tuvo usted otra actividad familiar favorita cuando creció?

© Harcourt

Name _____   Date _____

School-Home Connection

A Note to Family Members

What We Are Learning About Health

In Chapter 12 of *Harcourt Health and Fitness,* we are learning about

- identifying, preparing for, and protecting against potential natural disasters.
- using resources wisely to protect the health of the community and of the planet.
- setting goals in making plans and organizing actions that help the environment.
- making the school environment a pleasant place to spend time.

 Visit **www.harcourtschool.com/health** for links to parent resources.

How You Can Help

Parental involvement in the school environment is part of a coordinated school health plan that includes the home, school, community, and social services. You can support your school through increased communication and by volunteering your time or talents. At home you can support your child's learning by

- investigating some of the natural disasters that your community has been through.

- encouraging your child to come up with ways your family can help conserve resources.

- praising your child's efforts to make his or her school environment a better place.

A Family Activity

With your child, look through newspapers and news magazines to find articles about individuals and groups who have helped communities recover from natural disasters. Ask your child to choose his or her favorite article and summarize it in the spaces provided. Discuss why your child chose this article and what the article tells him or her about the importance of people helping people in times of trouble.

People Helping People

Who	
What	
When	
Where	
Why	

La escuela y la casa

Nota para los familiares

Lo que estamos aprendiendo acerca de la Salud

En el Capítulo 12 de *Harcourt Health and Fitness* estamos aprendiendo acerca de:

- Cómo identificar posibles desastres naturales y cómo prepararse para ellos.
- Cómo usar los recursos naturales adecuadamente para proteger la salud de la comunidad y del planeta.
- Cómo establecer metas al hacer planes y organizar campañas que ayuden a conservar el medio ambiente.
- Qué hacer para que el ambiente escolar sea agradable.

 Visite **www.harcourtschool.com/health** para encontrar enlaces con recursos en inglés para los padres.

Cómo puede usted ayudar

La participación familiar en las actividades escolares forma parte de un plan de salud organizado que incluye la casa, la escuela, la comunidad y los servicios sociales. Usted puede apoyar a la escuela manteniendo una buena comunicación y ofreciendo su tiempo y sus talentos como voluntario. En casa, usted puede apoyar el aprendizaje de su hijo(a) haciendo lo siguiente:

- Investiguen acerca de los desastres naturales que ha sufrido su comunidad.
- Anímelo a pensar en maneras en las que su familia puede ayudar a conservar los recursos naturales.
- Elógielo cuando se esfuerce por tratar de hacer que su ambiente escolar sea agradable.

Actividad familiar

Junto con su hijo(a), busque en periódicos y revistas artículos que hablen de personas y grupos que hayan ayudado a sus comunidades a recuperarse de desastres naturales. Pídale que elija su artículo favorito y que lo resuma en la tabla. Pídale que le diga por qué eligió ese artículo y qué dice acerca de la importancia de ayudarnos unos a otros en tiempos de crisis.

Personas ayudando a otras personas

Quién	
Qué	
Cuándo	
Dónde	
Por qué	

Writing Models

The writing models on the following pages are examples of writing for different purposes. Students can consult these models as they work on the writing assignments in the Lesson Summary and Reviews in *Harcourt Health and Fitness.* You may wish to distribute copies of the writing models for students to keep.

You will also find rubrics to use for scoring writing assignments. There are rubrics for Ideas/Content Organization, Sentence Fluency, Word Choice, Conventions, and Voice.

Write to Express

Write to Inform

Write to Entertain

© Harcourt

Writing in Health

Model: Business Letter

In a **business letter**, a writer may request information or express an opinion. A business letter has the same parts as a friendly letter, plus an inside address. This is the receiver's address. A business letter uses a colon after the words in the greeting, and the paragraphs are not indented.

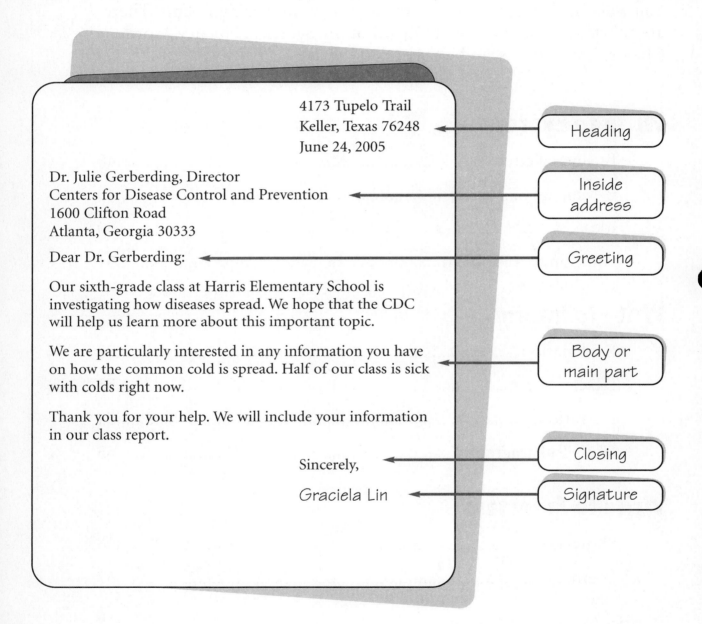

4173 Tupelo Trail
Keller, Texas 76248
June 24, 2005

Heading

Dr. Julie Gerberding, Director
Centers for Disease Control and Prevention
1600 Clifton Road
Atlanta, Georgia 30333

Inside address

Dear Dr. Gerberding:

Greeting

Our sixth-grade class at Harris Elementary School is investigating how diseases spread. We hope that the CDC will help us learn more about this important topic.

We are particularly interested in any information you have on how the common cold is spread. Half of our class is sick with colds right now.

Thank you for your help. We will include your information in our class report.

Body or main part

Sincerely,

Closing

Graciela Lin

Signature

Writing in Health

Model: E-Mail

Sending an **e-mail** is much like sending a letter. However, because it is being sent by computer, an e-mail should be short and to the point. You may wish to include a greeting and signature unless you are sure the receiver recognizes your e-mail address. Include a subject line to describe the content of your e-mail.

> Describe the subject of the message on the subject line. The computer automatically puts in the date.

Subj: Nutritional Information
Date: September 25, 2005
From: Smartkid3709@aox.com
To: nutrition@zxq.com

Please send me, by e-mail, information about your menu. I am interested in all breakfast, lunch, and dinner items.

I am most interested in the nutrients in all the menu choices. The amount of cholesterol in each of your food items is what I have the greatest need to know.

Thank you, in advance, for the information.

Sally French

> Be sure you have typed in the receiver's e-mail address correctly.

> Be sure your message is short and to the point.

Writing in Health

Model: Idea

An **idea** is a thought about something. Sometimes we decide to do or make something from an idea and then write about it. Choose a topic and tell how that idea came into your mind. Write the steps needed to carry out your idea. Tell whether your idea was a success.

Ready for the Storm

Because we live on Galveston Bay, our class is very aware of the beginning of hurricane season. In school, we learned how important a disaster kit can be when people are forced to evacuate their homes. When I learned that many of the people in my community could not afford a disaster kit, I had a great idea.

> What is your idea? How did you think of it?

With the help of my mom and our teacher, the class found that about three hundred families didn't have disaster kits. Of course, we couldn't afford to buy three hundred kits, so we put on our thinking caps to find supporters of my great idea.

Each kit had to contain the following: bottled water, canned and packaged food, a can opener, a portable radio, extra batteries, flashlights, first-aid supplies, blankets, and a plastic bucket.

Discount stores in our area agreed to supply all the items needed. Our class recruited members of other classes, and we set up an assembly line to assemble the kits.

> What steps did you take to carry out your idea?

Our next task was to figure out how to get the kits to the people who needed them. Then the Red Cross got involved and helped us distribute the kits.

A hurricane pounded our city just one month after we handed out the three hundred disaster kits. I had such a good feeling, knowing that we had helped others as a result of my great idea.

> Did your idea prove to be a good one? How did you feel in the end?

Writing in Health

Model: Solution to a Problem

Writing about a **solution to a problem** develops while you are thinking of alternative ways to solve the problem. Explore the advantages and disadvantages of a particular solution before you decide on it. Finally, determine how well the solution to the problem is working.

Floating for My Life

My family always enjoys spending weekends at the lake. One Saturday morning, instead of having fun, my mom was dialing 911 for someone to come and rescue me.

> What is the problem?

It was a clear, sunny day, and I could not wait to get into the water. My brother and I usually spend our time racing back and forth to the pier. This day, though, we lifted the buoys so that we could go beyond the designated swimming area.

I felt myself going under in a matter of seconds because I must have swum into an area that got deep fast. I knew that attempting to swim back to shore might take more energy than I had. My other option was to wait and see if someone noticed me. Either way, I knew I was in trouble. Because I was swimming with my brother, I decided that he might notice that I was no longer near him. I chose to begin survival floating.

> Weigh the advantages and disadvantages to find a solution.

We learned how to survival float in health class, but I never thought I would need it. I could hear my teacher's voice saying, "Lie on your stomach on the surface of the water." I held my breath, did that, put my face down, and let my arms and legs dangle. I stayed in the resting position until I needed to take a breath. Then I slowly raised my arms in front until they reached about shoulder height. I moved my legs so that one went forward and one went backwards. I pushed down with my arms and brought my legs together. This allowed my head to surface so that I could take a breath. I repeated this process until I saw the rescue team coming my way.

> Determine how well the solution worked.

I learned a lesson that day. I will never again swim into "no swimming" areas.

© Harcourt

Writing in Health

Model: Explanation

In an **explanation**, the writer helps the reader understand something. Use exact words to explain what something is, how it works, what happens during a process, or why something happens. Do not include your personal viewpoint in an explanation.

How to Have a Good Workout

We all know that getting enough exercise is important to staying healthy. Sometimes, however, if exercise is not done properly, the stress to the body could produce injuries. To prevent them, be sure to include a warm-up and a cool-down in your workouts.

The warm-up is vital because it slowly introduces your body to exercise. The heart rate and the respiration rate increase. As a result, more blood flows to the muscles, and the body temperature increases. Warming and stretching the muscles makes them more flexible. This helps you avoid injury.

When your body is warm and ready to go, get moving with an activity. Be sure to work out by doing something that you enjoy. Keep it going for twenty to thirty minutes. This can include any type of activity that will get your heart rate up and keep you moving.

After the workout, allow your body to return slowly to normal. Reduce the rate of the activity so that you are now working at a lower intensity. End with some cool-down stretches to prevent sore, stiff muscles.

A good workout can be a great workout when you do it properly and safely.

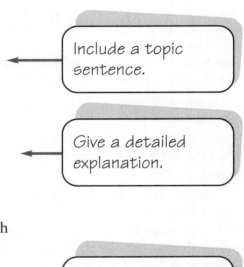

Include a topic sentence.

Give a detailed explanation.

Use exact words.

© Harcourt

Writing in Health

Model: Description

A **description** is writing that uses details to tell about a subject. You can also use figurative language and imagery to help the reader create a mental picture. You may also tell readers how you feel by giving your personal viewpoint.

Quick Thinking

I thought that baby-sitting my three-year-old neighbor, Olivia, and her seven-year-old sister, Kristy, was sure to be easy money. Little did I know that, if not for my quick thinking and knowledge of a life-saving technique, little Olivia would not be here today.

> Describe your **topic** in a main idea sentence.

To relieve the monotony of the day, we took a stroll around the neighborhood. We stopped at the park to allow Kristy time to fly with the birds as she soared into the air on the swing. I could hear her loud squeals of delight.

> Use **figurative language**.

After the three of us agreed that it was time for a snack, we stopped at the corner store to buy some candy. Kristy bought a bag of little, round, hard candies. She said those were her favorites. Olivia bought chocolate since she could not eat Kristy's candy, which was a potential choking hazard.

When we got back to the girl's house, I was looking at the television guide for a program both girls would enjoy. It was then I heard Kristy shout that something was wrong.

I looked up and saw Olivia with her hands around her throat: the universal choking sign. I heard no gasping for air or crying for help. I knew that something was lodged in her throat. Without hesitation, I pulled the fragile little girl closer to me so that her back was facing me. I put my arms around her waist and my fist above her belly button. Then I grabbed the fist with my other hand. I pulled my hands toward me and gave five quick, hard, upward thrusts on Olivia's stomach.

I heard a smack against the wall like a baseball hitting a bat. I looked up and quickly glanced at Kristy. Olivia began to cry. "What just happened?" I asked.

> Use **imagery**.

I saw the tears rolling down Kristy's cheeks. "It's one of the little, round, hard candies I bought. Olivia wanted to try a piece, and I thought it would be okay."

I do not imagine that Kristy or I will ever forget the sound of the candy hitting the wall as it was ejected from Olivia's throat. Olivia smiled and gave me a big hug. Somehow, she knew I had done something special for her.

> Express your **personal viewpoint**.

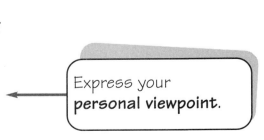

© Harcourt

Writing in Health

Model: Narration

A **personal narrative** is a story about the writer's own experiences. The writer often tells about a lesson he or she learned or a significant event that helped the writer understand something differently.

Too Stuffed for My Own Good

I am a typical sixth-grader. I talk on the phone a lot. I watch more TV than my mom likes. And I snack on junk food while I do both of these activities.

> Introduce the writer.

It never occurred to me that this lifestyle did not promote good health since my usual after-school routine made me feel satisfied, although not energetic. I noticed that my clothes were getting a little tight, and when Mom and I went shopping, I had to buy a larger size. I told myself, however, that I was just getting a little taller, which was really true. I ignored the fact that I was also getting a little wider.

This sedentary lifestyle and constant snacking came to a screeching halt after Mom's doctor told her that *she* needed to change *her* eating habits to make her heart healthier. My mom came home one day and tossed all the junk food in the trash. "But it's such a waste of food and money!" I said.

> Describe the event that caused the writer to change.

"Our health is more important than that junk!" replied Mom.

By this time the trash bag was spilling over with corn chips, potato chips, and caramel corn. The pantry was emptied of its stockpile of food ready for emergency snacking. Down the garbage disposal went the French onion dip.

We dusted off our bicycles and canceled the lawn service. Mom thought we could all use a little exercise. For dinner, my mom now plans our meals according to the Food Guide Pyramid. Also, we have to limit our phone calls to ten minutes. Because my brother and I joined a soccer team, we're now too busy to talk on the phone!

> Tell how the event changed the writer.

What is really surprising is that my family has a lot more fun together now. And, I must admit, I have a lot more energy when I get home from school.

Writing Model

Writing in Health

Model: How-To Paragraph

In **how-to paragraphs**, a writer gives a systematic explanation of how to make or do something. List all the materials you will need for the activity. Write the steps in a logical order.

How to Check Your Target Heart Rate

Playing soccer, jumping rope, and participating in other kinds of strenuous recreational activities are not only enjoyable, these activities can also contribute to a stronger heart and lungs. How can you be sure your heart and lungs are getting the benefits of exercise? You need to measure your target heart rate. To do this, you will need a timepiece to count the number of heartbeats.

First, choose an activity that you know will get your heart pumping. Then, in the middle of your workout, find your pulse at your wrist or neck. Next, use the timepiece to count the number of beats in six seconds. Add a zero to that number. This is your heart rate. Finally, if you are under 20 and your heart rate is lower than 145, exercise harder to get above 145 and into the target heart rate zone. If your heart rate is higher than 185, you should slow down. You do not want your heart working too hard!

If you really want to benefit from these activities, be sure to stay in your target heart rate zone for at least 20 minutes. Not only will you have a great time with your friends, you will also be doing your heart and lungs a healthy favor!

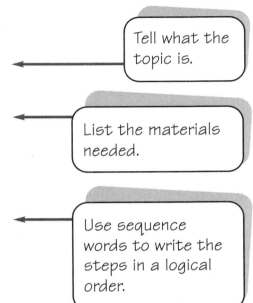

Tell what the topic is.

List the materials needed.

Use sequence words to write the steps in a logical order.

Writing in Health

Model: Story

A **story** is writing that includes characters, a setting, and a plot. The characters in a story can be real or imaginary. The main character in a story has a problem to solve. Tell the events of the story in the order that they happen.

Stressed to the Max

I consider myself a capable member of the sixth grade. In spite of that, my world almost collapsed the morning that my report on Egypt was due. It all started with a key.

My mom always leaves for work earlier than I leave for school, so it is my job to lock the house. I turn the lock on the knob with a flick of the finger and sprint to the bus stop. On this particular day, I turned the lock on the knob, took two steps towards the bus, and abruptly stopped, realizing that I forgot to take the report I painstakingly wrote during the night.

With a sinking feeling in my stomach, I reached into my pocket for the house key and then visualized it still sitting on the table next to my report. My palms started to sweat, and now I felt my stomach churning. I was locked out of the house and did not have access to all my hard work that lay on the kitchen table.

My mom had given me a cell phone for emergencies, and without a doubt, this qualified as an emergency in my book. But my mom could not "save the day," because she was in a meeting all day. I could feel my mouth getting dry and my heart beating faster. I was stressed. I knew that facing my teacher was going to be very uncomfortable.

As I walked into the classroom, I took a deep breath and exhaled slowly. I focused on telling my teacher exactly what had happened. "Oh my," said Mrs. Taylor. "I've locked myself out of my apartment at times, and it's a dreadful feeling. Let's plan to hear your report tomorrow."

"That works for me," I said, with a sigh of relief.

I did say that my world *almost* collapsed. One thing you can count on in a stressful situation: things usually get better.

> Use elaboration to give details about the characters.

> Use exact words to tell about the problem that the character has to solve.

> Give the events of the story in time order.

Writing in Health

Model: Poem

A **poem** is a way for a writer to describe something or express feelings about a subject. Word choice is important, and so are rhythm and rhyme. Poems often use figures of speech, such as similes and metaphors, to help "paint a word picture" for the reader.

Forever Friendships

Title

I had a friend in second grade.
Her name was Gloria McVay.
I said to her, "You're my best friend.
We'll be best friends, 'til the end, 'til the end."

But when I moved to a different state,
my best friend was now named Kate.
Kate was as smart as a third grader gets,
Her brain was like a sponge, and she was fun, you can bet.

Simile

The news was devastating that came through one day:
Our school would be rezoned without delay.
Now, Kate's school was located across our town,
So there I was, feeling alone and down.

Vivid Words

What's a girl to do when her best friend leaves?
We did everything together; we were as thick as thieves!
Kate and I vowed not to lose track,
even though we realized she couldn't move back.

Rhyme

So, I have a friend that I'll keep forever,
through high school, college, every endeavor.
Even in junior high, when I'm in the school band,
you never know what new friends I'll land.

Sometimes friendships are really quite fleeting,
However, forever friends are truly worth meeting.

Rubrics for Writing Practice

A Six-Point Scoring Scale

Student work produced for writing assessment can be scored by using a six-point scale. Although each rubric includes specific descriptors for each score point, each score can also be framed in a more global perspective.

SCORE OF 6: EXEMPLARY. Writing at this level is both exceptional and memorable. It is often characterized by distinctive and unusually sophisticated thought processes, rich details, and outstanding craftsmanship.

SCORE OF 5: STRONG. Writing at this level exceeds the standard. It is thorough and complex, and it consistently portrays exceptional control of content and skills.

SCORE OF 4: PROFICIENT. Writing at this level meets the standard. It is solid work that has more strengths than weaknesses. The writing demonstrates mastery of skills and reflects considerable care and commitment.

SCORE OF 3: DEVELOPING. Writing at this level shows basic, although sometimes inconsistent, mastery and application of content and skills. It shows some strengths but tends to have more weaknesses overall.

SCORE OF 2: EMERGING. Writing at this level is often superficial, fragmented, or incomplete. It may show a partial mastery of content and skills, but it needs considerable development before reflecting the proficient level of performance.

SCORE OF 1: BEGINNING. Writing at this level is minimal. It typically lacks understanding and use of appropriate skills and strategies. The writing may contain major errors.

Rubric for Ideas/Content

Score	Description
6	The writing is exceptionally clear, focused, and interesting. It holds the reader's attention throughout. Main ideas stand out and are developed by strong support and rich details suitable to the audience and the purpose.
5	The writing is clear, focused, and interesting. It holds the reader's attention. Main ideas stand out and are developed by supporting details suitable to the audience and the purpose.
4	The writing is clear and focused. The reader can easily understand the main ideas. Support is present, although it may be limited or rather general.
3	The reader can understand the main ideas, although they may be overly broad or simplistic, and the results may not be effective. Supporting details are often limited, insubstantial, overly general, or occasionally slightly off topic.
2	The main ideas and purpose are somewhat unclear, or development is attempted but minimal.
1	The writing lacks a central idea or purpose.

Rubric for Organization

Score	Description
6	The organization enhances the central idea(s) and its development. The order and structure are compelling and move the reader through the text easily.
5	The organization enhances the central idea(s) and its development. The order and structure are strong and move the reader through the text.
4	The organization is clear and coherent. Order and structure are present but may seem formulaic.
3	An attempt has been made to organize the writing; however, the overall structure is inconsistent or skeletal.
2	The writing lacks a clear organizational structure. An occasional organizational device is discernible; however, either the writing is difficult to follow and the reader has to reread substantial portions, or the piece is simply too short to demonstrate organizational skills.
1	The writing lacks coherence; organization seems haphazard and disjointed. Even after rereading, the reader remains confused.

© Harcourt

Student _____ Date _____

Evaluator _____

Rubric for Sentence Fluency

Score	Description
6	The writing has an effective flow and rhythm. Sentences show a high degree of craftsmanship, with consistently strong and varied structure that makes expressive oral reading easy and enjoyable.
5	The writing has an easy flow and rhythm. Sentences are carefully crafted, with strong and varied structure that makes expressive oral reading easy and enjoyable.
4	The writing flows; however, connections between phrases or sentences may be less than fluid. Sentence patterns are somewhat varied, contributing to ease in oral reading.
3	The writing tends to be mechanical rather than fluid. Occasional awkward constructions may force the reader to slow down or reread.
2	The writing tends to be either choppy or rambling. Awkward constructions often force the reader to slow down or reread.
1	The writing is difficult to follow or to read aloud. Sentences tend to be incomplete, rambling, or very awkward.

Rubric for Word Choice

Score	Description
6	The words convey the intended message in an exceptionally interesting, precise, and natural way appropriate to the audience and the purpose. The writer employs a rich, broad range of words that have been carefully chosen and thoughtfully placed for impact.
5	The words convey the intended message in an interesting, precise, and natural way appropriate to the audience and the purpose. The writer employs a broad range of words that have been carefully chosen and thoughtfully placed for impact.
4	The words effectively convey the intended message. The writer employs a variety of words that are functional and appropriate to the audience and the purpose.
3	The language is quite ordinary, lacking interest, precision, and variety, or may be inappropriate to the audience and the purpose in places. The writer does not employ a variety of words, producing a sort of "generic" paper filled with familiar words and phrases.
2	The language is monotonous and/or misused, detracting from the meaning and impact.
1	The writing shows an extremely limited vocabulary or is so filled with misuses of words that the meaning is obscured. Because of vague or imprecise language, only the most general kind of message is communicated.

© Harcourt

60 • Writing Rubrics   **Teaching Resources**

Rubric for Conventions

Score	Description
6	The writing demonstrates exceptionally strong control of standard writing conventions (e.g., punctuation, spelling, capitalization, paragraph breaks, grammar, and usage) and uses them effectively to enhance communication. Errors are so few and so minor that the reader can easily skim right over them unless specifically searching for them.
5	The writing demonstrates strong control of standard writing conventions (e.g., punctuation, spelling, capitalization, paragraph breaks, grammar, and usage) and uses them effectively to enhance communication. Errors are so few and so minor that they do not impede readability.
4	The writing demonstrates control of standard writing conventions (e.g., punctuation, spelling, capitalization, paragraph breaks, grammar, and usage). Minor errors, while perhaps noticeable, do not impede readability.
3	The writing demonstrates limited control of standard writing conventions (e.g., punctuation, spelling, capitalization, paragraph breaks, grammar, and usage). Errors begin to impede readability.
2	The writing demonstrates little control of standard writing conventions. Frequent, significant errors impede readability.
1	Numerous errors in usage, spelling, capitalization, and punctuation repeatedly distract the reader and make the text difficult to read. In fact, the severity and frequency of errors are so overwhelming that the reader finds it difficult to focus on the message and must reread for meaning.

Rubric for Voice

Score	Description
6	The writer has chosen a voice appropriate for the topic, purpose, and audience. The writer seems deeply committed to the topic, and there is an exceptional sense of "writing to be read." The writing is expressive, engaging, or sincere.
5	The writer has chosen a voice appropriate for the topic, purpose, and audience. The writer seems committed to the topic, and there is a sense of "writing to be read." The writing is expressive, engaging, or sincere.
4	A voice is present. The writer demonstrates commitment to the topic, and there may be a sense of "writing to be read." In places the writing is expressive, engaging, or sincere.
3	The writer's commitment to the topic seems inconsistent. A sense of the writer may emerge at times; however, the voice is either inappropriately personal or inappropriately impersonal.
2	The writing provides little sense of involvement or commitment. There is no evidence that the writer has chosen a suitable voice.
1	The writing seems to lack a sense of involvement or commitment.

Identify Cause and Effect

Cause:

Effect:

Reading Skill Graphic Organizer

Compare and Contrast

Topic:

Alike

Different

Draw Conclusions

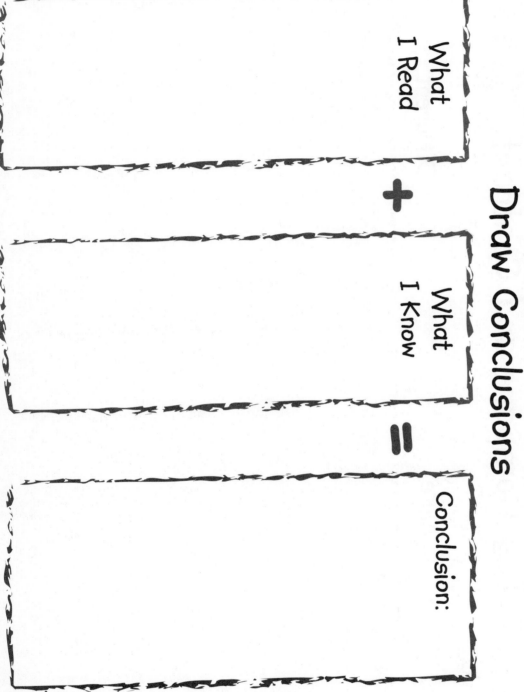

What
I Read

+

What
I Know

=

Conclusion:

Identify Main Idea and Details

Main Idea:

Detail:

Detail:

Detail:

Sequence

1.

2.

3.

Reading Skill Graphic Organizer

Summarize

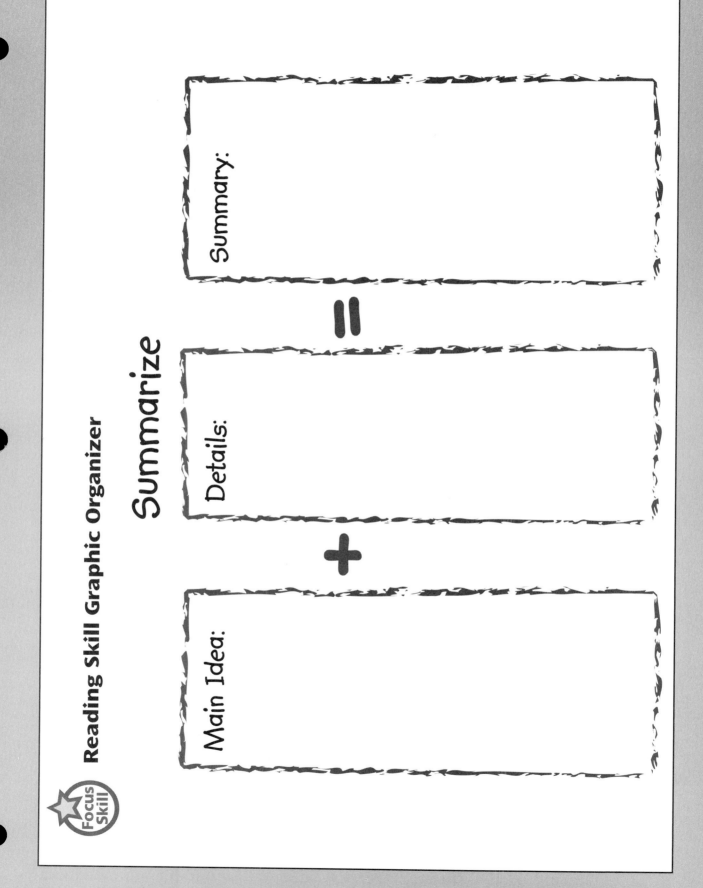

Summary:

=

Details:

+

Main Idea:

Focus Skill

Preview Vocabulary

Words I Know

Words I've Seen or Heard

New Words

Venn Diagram

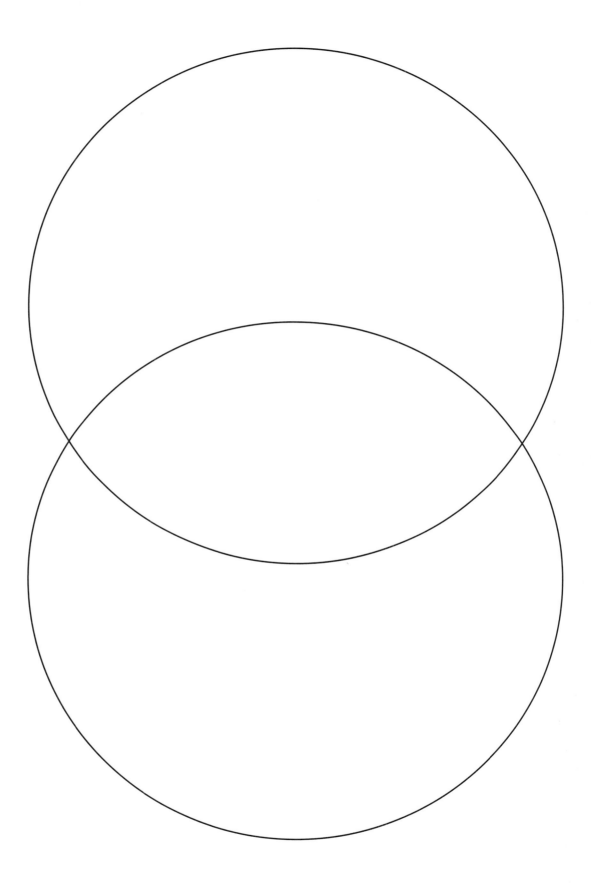

K-W-L Chart

What I Know	What I Want to Know	What I Learned

Web

Chart

Knowledge Chart

Topic _____

Prior Knowledge	New Knowledge
1.	1.
2.	2.
3.	3.
4.	4.
5.	5.
6.	6.
7.	7.

© Harcourt

Project Plan

What I Want to Find Out

1.

How I Can Find Out

2.

What I Need to Do

3.

Materials

How I Can Share Information

4.

Introduction to the Health and Safety Handbook

Using the Health and Safety Handbook

This section of *Teaching Resources* provides information that addresses important health concerns for students, such as nutrition, physical fitness, safety, and first aid. In addition, it identifies life skills and character traits that are learned early in life and are used in daily interaction with others. This section is intended to supplement and extend the content of the *Student Edition.*

In the Classroom

You can use these pages as stand-alone lessons. You may wish to make copies of these pages for students to compile in a personal health and safety handbook as you teach core lessons from the *Student Edition.*

At Home

You may wish to send copies of these pages home so that students can discuss the tips and topics with their families. The copies can also serve as a reference if students are completing health projects at home.

Health and Safety Handbook
Contents

Understanding Life Skills

Having good health isn't just knowing the facts about what to eat or how to stay well. It's also thinking critically about those facts and knowing how to apply them to your daily life. Using life skills to apply your growing health knowledge can help you reach the goal of good health.

Communicate

In order to communicate well, you need to explain your ideas, needs, or feelings in a way that others can understand. You also need to listen to and try to understand what others have to say.

Steps for Communicating

1. Understand your audience.
2. Give a clear message.
3. Listen carefully, and answer any questions.
4. Gather feedback.

Ways to Give a Clear Message

- Use "I" messages.
- Use a respectful tone of voice.
- Make eye contact.
- Use appropriate body language.
- Express ideas in a clear, organized way.

Make Responsible Decisions

When you make decisions, you think about a group of choices and decide on the wisest thing to do in order to avoid risky situations or health risks.

Steps for Making Decisions

1. Find out about the choices you could make.
2. Eliminate choices that are illegal or against your family rules.
3. Ask yourself: What is the possible result of each choice? Does the choice show good character?
4. Decide on what seems to be the best choice.

Understanding Life Skills

Manage Stress

Everyone feels stress. Knowing how to manage your stress can help you get through tense or exciting situations.

Steps for Managing Stress

1. Know what stress feels like and what causes it.

2. Try to determine the cause of the stress.

3. Do something that will help you relieve the feelings of stress.

Ways to Relieve Stress

- Do deep breathing and muscle relaxing exercises.

- Take a walk, exercise, or play a sport.

- Talk to someone you trust about the way you're feeling.

- Watch a funny movie or television show.

- Do something creative such as write, dance, or draw.

Refuse

Knowing what to say *before* you are asked to do something you don't want to do can keep you moving toward good health.

How to Refuse

- Say **no** firmly, and state your reasons for saying **no**.

- Remember a consequence, and keep saying **no**.

- Suggest something else to do.

- Repeat **no**, and walk away. Leave the door open for the other person to join you.

Other Ways to Refuse

- Continue to repeat **no**.

- Change the subject.

- Avoid possible problem situations.

- Ignore the person. Give him or her the "cold shoulder."

- Stay with people who also refuse to do unhealthful actions.

- Reverse the peer pressure.

- Use humor or any other nonviolent way that works.

Understanding Life Skills

Resolve Conflicts

You must choose and use strategies to communicate and compromise in order to find solutions to problems or to avoid violence.

Steps for Resolving Conflicts

1. Use "I" messages to tell how you feel.

2. Listen to the other person. Consider the other person's point of view.

3. Talk about a solution.

4. Find a way for both sides to win.

Ways to Talk About a Solution

- Negotiate.

- Ask for a mediator.

- Take a break until everyone cools down.

- Make a decision by consensus.

- Use humor if appropriate.

Set Goals

When you set goals, you must decide on a change you want to make and then take actions to make that change happen.

Steps for Setting Goals

1. Choose a goal.

2. Plan steps to meet the goal. Determine whether you will need any help.

3. Check your progress as you work toward the goal.

4. Reflect on and evaluate your progress toward the goal.

Building Good Character

Caring	Citizenship	Fairness	Respect	Responsibility	Trustworthiness

These are values we choose to help guide us in our daily living. The rules that come from these values are the ground rules of good behavior.

Caring

"It is one of the most beautiful compensations of life, that no man can sincerely try to help another without helping himself."

—Ralph Waldo Emerson

DO
- Support and value family members.
- Be a good friend and share your feelings.
- Show concern for others.
- Thank people who help you.
- Help people in need.

DON'T
- Don't be selfish.
- Don't expect rewards for being caring.
- Don't gossip.
- Don't hurt anyone's feelings.

How do YOU show CARING?

Citizenship

"We must learn to live together as brothers or perish together as fools."

—Martin Luther King, Jr.

DO
- Take pride in your school, community, state, and country.
- Obey laws and rules and respect authority.
- Be a good neighbor.
- Help keep your school and neighborhood safe and clean.
- Cooperate with others.
- Protect the environment.

DON'T
- Don't break rules and laws.
- Don't waste natural resources.
- Don't damage public property or the property of others.
- Don't litter or hurt the environment in other ways.

How do YOU show CITIZENSHIP?

Health and Safety Handbook

Building Good Character

| Caring | Citizenship | Fairness | Respect | Responsibility | Trustworthiness |

These are values we choose to help guide us in our daily living. The rules that come from these values are the ground rules of good behavior.

Fairness

"Justice cannot be for one side alone, but must be for both."

—**Eleanor Roosevelt**

DO
- Play by the rules.
- Be a good sport.
- Share.
- Take turns.
- Listen to the opinions of others.

DON'T
- Don't take more than your share.
- Don't be a bad loser or a bad winner.
- Don't take advantage of others.
- Don't blame others without cause.
- Don't cut in front of others in line.

How do YOU show FAIRNESS?

Respect

"I believe . . . that every human mind feels pleasure in doing good to another."

—**Thomas Jefferson**

DO
- Treat others the way you want to be treated.
- Accept people who are different from you.
- Be polite and use good manners.
- Be considerate of the feelings of others.
- Stay calm when you are angry.
- Develop self-respect and self-confidence.

DON'T
- Don't use bad language.
- Don't insult or embarrass anyone.
- Don't threaten or bully anyone.
- Don't hit or hurt anyone.

How do YOU show RESPECT?

© Harcourt

Building Good Character

| Caring | Citizenship | Fairness | Respect | Responsibility | Trustworthiness |

These are values we choose to help guide us in our daily living. The rules that come from these values are the ground rules of good behavior.

Responsibility

"Responsibility is the price of greatness."

—Winston Churchill

DO
- Practice self-control and self-discipline.
- Express feelings, needs, and wants in appropriate ways.
- Practice good health habits.
- Keep yourself safe.
- Keep trying. Do your best.
- Complete tasks.
- Set goals and carry them out.
- Be a good role model.

DON'T
- Don't smoke. Don't use alcohol or other drugs.
- Don't do things that are unsafe or destructive.
- Don't be swayed by negative peer pressure.
- Don't deny or make excuses for your mistakes.
- Don't leave your work for others to do.
- Don't lose or misuse your belongings.

How do YOU show RESPONSIBILITY?

Trustworthiness

"What you do speaks so loudly that I cannot hear what you say."

—Ralph Waldo Emerson

DO
- Be honest. Tell the truth.
- Do the right thing.
- Report dangerous situations.
- Be dependable.
- Be loyal to your family, friends, and country.
- Take care of things you borrow, and return them promptly.

DON'T
- Don't tell lies.
- Don't cheat.
- Don't steal.
- Don't break promises.
- Don't borrow without asking first.

How do YOU show TRUSTWORTHINESS?

Good Nutrition

The Food Guide Pyramid

No one food or food group supplies all the nutrients you need. That's why it's important to eat a variety of foods from all the food groups. The Food Guide Pyramid can help you choose healthful foods in the right amounts. By choosing more foods from the groups at the bottom of the pyramid and few foods from the group at the top, you will eat nutrient-rich foods that provide your body with energy to grow and develop.

The number of servings from each food group is suggested for children ages 7–12.

Fats, oils, and sweets
Eat sparingly.

Milk, yogurt, and cheese
3 servings

Meat, poultry, fish, dried beans, eggs, and nuts 2–3 servings

Vegetables
3–5 servings

Fruit
2–4 servings

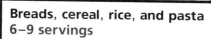

Breads, cereal, rice, and pasta
6–9 servings

© Harcourt

Good Nutrition

More Food Guide Pyramids

The Food Guide Pyramid from the United States Department of Agriculture, or USDA, (page 83) shows common foods from the United States. Foods from different cultures and lifestyles also can make up a healthful diet. The other pyramids shown here can help you to add interesting new foods to your diet.

Vegetarians (vej·uh·TAIR·ee·uhnz) are people who choose not to eat any meat, poultry, or fish. Some vegetarians also choose to avoid dairy products and eggs. A balanced vegetarian diet is just as healthful as a balanced diet that includes meats.

Vegetarian

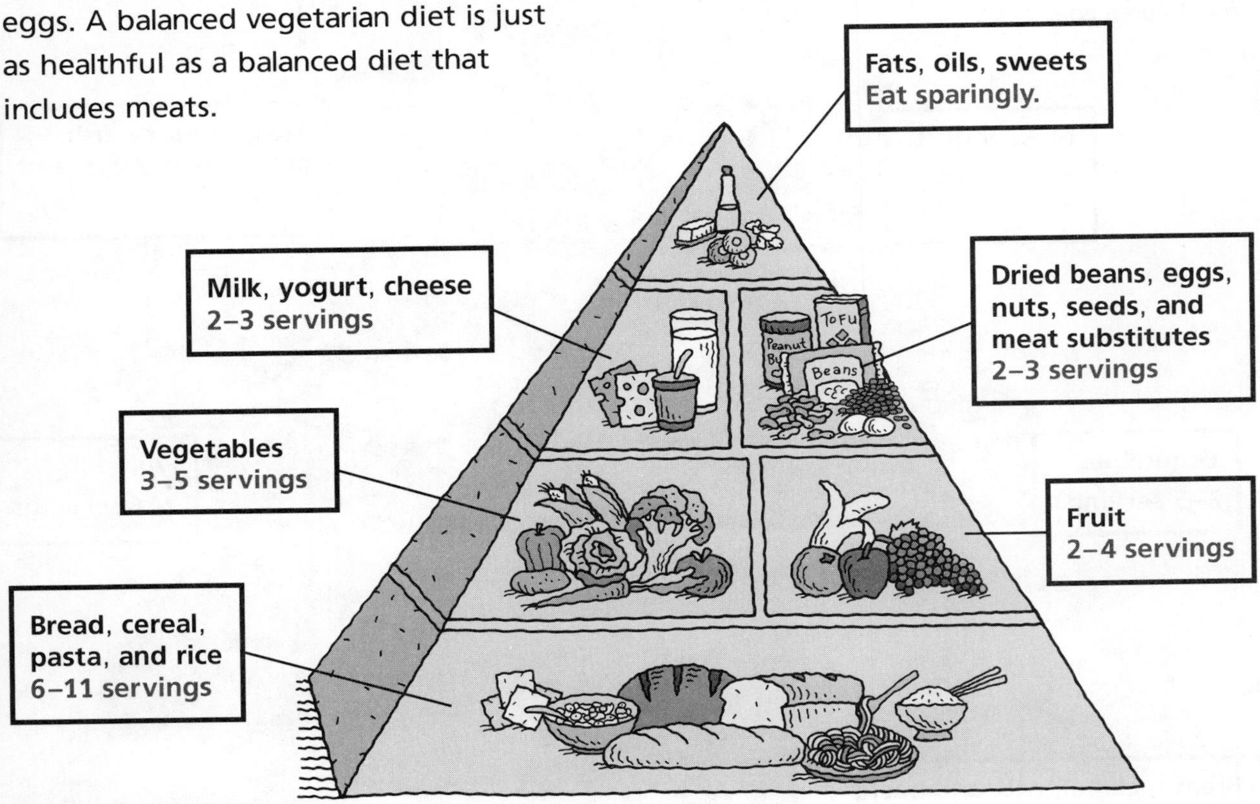

Fats, oils, sweets
Eat sparingly.
Milk, yogurt, cheese
2–3 servings
Dried beans, eggs, nuts, seeds, and meat substitutes
2–3 servings
Vegetables
3–5 servings
Fruit
2–4 servings
Bread, cereal, pasta, and rice
6–11 servings
Tofu
Peanut Butter
Beans

The number of servings from each food group is suggested for adults.

The tops of these two pyramids differ from the one on page 83. They suggest eating seafood, poultry, eggs, and meat each week or month rather than each day. Moderate daily use of vegetable oils is also recommended. What other differences do you notice?

Asian

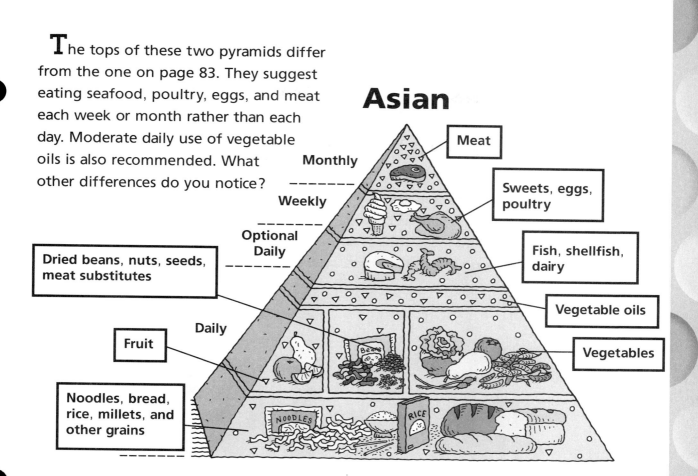

Monthly
- - - - - - -
Weekly
- - - - - - -
Optional Daily
- - - - - - -
Daily

Meat

Sweets, eggs, poultry

Fish, shellfish, dairy

Vegetable oils

Vegetables

Dried beans, nuts, seeds, meat substitutes

Fruit

Noodles, bread, rice, millets, and other grains

Mediterranean

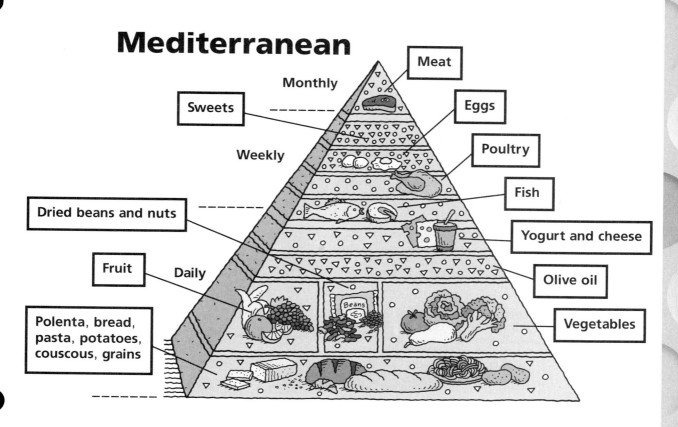

Monthly
- - - - - - -
Weekly
- - - - - - -
Daily

Meat

Sweets

Eggs

Poultry

Fish

Yogurt and cheese

Olive oil

Vegetables

Dried beans and nuts

Fruit

Polenta, bread, pasta, potatoes, couscous, grains

© Harcourt

Good Nutrition

Dietary Guidelines for Americans

These guidelines come from the USDA. They promote good nutrition and healthful choices. Following them will help you make choices about nutrition and health. Making the right choices will help you feel your best.

Aim for Fitness

- Aim for a healthful weight. Find out your healthful weight range from a health professional. If you need to, set goals to reach a better weight.

- Be physically active each day. (Use the Activity Pyramid on page 100 to help you.)

Health and Safety Handbook

Build a Healthful Base

- Use a food guide pyramid to guide your food choices.

- Each day, choose a variety of grains, such as wheat, oats, rice, and corn. Choose whole grains when you can.

- Each day, choose a variety of fruits and vegetables.

- Keep food safe to eat. (Follow the tips on pages 89 and 92 for safely preparing and storing food.)

Choose Sensibly

- Choose a diet that is moderate in total fat and low in saturated fat and cholesterol.

- Choose foods and drinks that are low in sugar. Lower the amount of sugar you eat.

- Choose foods that are low in salt. When you prepare foods, use very little salt.

Good Nutrition
Estimating Serving Size

The Food Guide Pyramid suggests a number of daily servings to eat from each group. But a serving isn't necessarily the amount you eat at a meal. A plate full of macaroni and cheese may contain three or four servings of bread (macaroni) and three servings of cheese. That's about half your bread servings and all your milk-group servings at one sitting! The table below can help you estimate the number of servings you are eating.

Food Group	Amount of Food in One Serving	Easy Ways to Estimate Serving Size
Bread, Cereal, Rice, and Pasta Group	$\frac{1}{2}$ cup cooked pasta, rice, or cereal I slice bread, $\frac{1}{2}$ bagel I cup ready-to-eat (dry) cereal	ice-cream scoop
Vegetable Group	I cup raw leafy vegetables $\frac{1}{2}$ cup other vegetables, cooked or chopped raw $\frac{1}{2}$ cup tomato sauce	about the size of a tennis ball
Fruit Group	I medium apple, pear, or orange I medium banana $\frac{1}{2}$ cup chopped or cooked fruit I cup fresh fruit 4 oz fruit juice	about the size of a baseball
Milk, Yogurt, and Cheese Group	$1\frac{1}{2}$ oz cheese 8 oz yogurt 8 oz milk	about the size of three dominoes
Meat, Poultry, Fish, Dried Beans, Eggs, and Nuts Group	2–3 oz lean meat, chicken, or fish 2 tablespoons peanut butter $\frac{1}{2}$ cup cooked dry beans	about the size of a computer mouse
Fats, Oils, and Sweets Group	I teaspoon margarine or butter	about the size of the end of your thumb

© Harcourt

Preparing Foods Safely

Fight Bacteria

You probably already know to throw away food that smells bad or looks moldy. But food doesn't have to look or smell bad to make you ill. To keep your food safe and yourself from becoming ill, follow the steps outlined in the picture below. And remember—when in doubt, throw it out!

FIGHT BAC!

Keep Food Safe From Bacteria ®

CLEAN
Wash hands and surfaces often.

SEPARATE
Don't cross-contaminate.

CHILL
Refrigerate promptly.

COOK
Cook to proper temperatures.

Preparing Foods Safely
Kitchen Safety

Sometimes you may cook a meal or prepare a snack for yourself. Be careful—kitchens can be dangerous. You need to follow safety rules to avoid burns, cuts, and other accidental injuries. You should be especially careful if you're home by yourself.

General Rules

- Follow rules for preparing and storing food safely (page 92).

- Be sure a responsible adult knows what you plan to cook and which kitchen tools you will use.

- Learn fire safety rules for the home.

- To avoid the risk of burns and fires, use the stove and oven as little as possible.

- Clean up after yourself. Turn off all appliances before you leave the kitchen.

Monday	Tuesday	Wednesday	Thursday	Friday
apple	cheese and crackers	banana	milk and granola	low-fat yogurt

Stoves and Ovens

- Get an adult's permission to use the stove or oven. If possible, use a microwave instead.

- Keep clothing away from burners. Avoid clothes with sleeves or laces that hang down; they could catch fire.

- Keep pot handles turned in toward the center of the stove.

- Use an oven mitt to handle hot trays or metal pot handles. A mitt covers your whole hand.

- Be sure you have a firm grip before you lift a container of hot food.

Microwaves

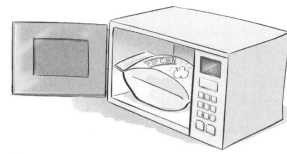

Always follow the directions on the food label. Remember these rules:

- Be careful when you take food out of a microwave. Even if the container isn't hot, steam can burn you.

- Never use metal containers, dishes with gold or silver decoration, or aluminum foil in a microwave. The metal can cause sparks or even start a fire.

- Never use a microwave to heat only water. When heating water, always place a non-metal object such as a wooden stirrer in the container.

Appliances and Kitchen Tools

- Check with an adult to find out which appliances you are allowed to use.

- Never turn an appliance off or on while your hands are wet.

- Kitchen knives are sharp and very dangerous. You should use knives and other sharp kitchen tools only with an adult's permission.

Food Safety Tips

Tips for Preparing Food

- Wash your hands thoroughly before preparing food. Also wash your hands after preparing each dish.

- Defrost meat in a microwave or the refrigerator. Do NOT defrost meat on the kitchen counter.

- Keep raw meat, poultry, and fish and their juices away from other food.

- Wash cutting boards, knives, and countertops immediately after cutting up meat, poultry, or fish. Never use the same cutting board for meats and vegetables without thoroughly washing the board first.

Tips for Cooking Food

- Cook all food thoroughly, especially meat. This will kill bacteria that can make you ill.

- Red meats should be cooked to a temperature of 160°F. Poultry should be cooked to 180°F. When fish is safely cooked, it flakes easily with a fork.

- Eggs should be cooked until the yolks are firm. Never eat foods or drink anything containing raw eggs. Never eat uncooked cookie dough made with raw eggs.

Tips for Cleaning Up the Kitchen

- Wash all dishes, utensils, and countertops with hot, soapy water.

- Store leftovers in small containers that will cool quickly in the refrigerator. Don't leave leftovers on the counter to cool.

- Your refrigerator should be 40°F or colder.

- Write the date on leftovers. Don't store them for more than five days.

Health and Safety Handbook

Being Physically Active
Guidelines for a Good Workout

There are three things you should do every time you are going to exercise—warm up, work out, and cool down.

Warm Up: When you warm up, your heartbeat rate, respiration rate, and body temperature gradually increase and more blood begins to flow to your muscles. As your body warms up, your flexibility increases, helping you avoid muscle stiffness after exercising. People who warm up are also less likely to have exercise-related injuries. Your warm-up should include five minutes of stretching and five minutes of a low-level form of your workout exercise. For example, if you are going to run for your primary exercise, you should spend five minutes stretching, concentrating on your legs and lower back, and five minutes walking before you start running. Some simple stretches are shown on pages 98–99.

Work Out: The main part of your exercise routine should be an aerobic exercise that lasts twenty to thirty minutes. Some common aerobic exercises include walking, bicycling, jogging, swimming, cross-country skiing, jumping rope, dancing, and playing racket sports. You should choose an activity that is fun for you and that you will enjoy doing over a long period of time. You may want to mix up the types of activities you do. This helps you work different muscle groups and provides a better overall workout. Some common aerobic exercises are shown on pages 94–95.

Cool Down: When you finish your aerobic exercise, you need to give your body time to return to normal. You also need to stretch again. This portion of your workout is called a cool-down. Start your cool-down with three to five minutes of low-level activity. For example, if you have been running, you may want to jog and then walk during this time. Then do stretching exercises to prevent soreness and stiffness.

Being Physically Active
Building a Strong Heart and Lungs

Aerobic activities, those that cause deep breathing and a fast heartbeat rate for at least twenty minutes, help both your heart and your lungs. Because your heart is a muscle, it gets stronger with exercise. A strong heart doesn't have to work as hard to pump blood to the rest of your body. Exercise also allows your lungs to hold more air. With a strong heart and lungs, your cells get oxygen faster and your body works more efficiently.

◀ **Swimming** Swimming may provide the best overall body workout of any sport. It uses all the major muscle groups and improves flexibility. The risk of injury is low, because the water supports your weight, greatly reducing stress on the joints. Just be sure to swim only when a lifeguard is present.

▶ **In-Line Skating** In-line skating gives your heart and lungs a great workout. Remember to always wear a helmet when skating. Always wear protective pads on your elbows and knees, and guards on your wrists, too. Learning how to skate, stop, and fall correctly will reduce your chance of injury.

© Harcourt

▶ **Tennis** To get the best aerobic workout from tennis, you should run as fast, far, and hard as you can during the game. Move away from the ball so that you can step into it as you hit it. Finally, try to involve your entire body in every move.

◀ **Walking** A fast-paced walk is a terrific way to build your endurance. The only equipment you need is a good pair of shoes and clothes appropriate for the weather. Walking with a friend can make this exercise a lot of fun.

▶ **Bicycling** Bicycling provides good aerobic activity that places little stress on the joints. It's also a great way to see the countryside. Be sure to use a bike that fits and to learn and follow the rules of the road. And *always* wear your helmet!

© Harcourt

Health and Safety Handbook

Being Physically Active
The President's Challenge

The President's Challenge is a physical fitness program designed for students ages 6 to 17. It's made up of five activities that promote physical fitness. Each participant receives an emblem patch and a certificate signed by the President.

The Five Awards

 Presidential Physical Fitness Award—presented to students scoring in the top 15 percent in all events.

 National Physical Fitness Award—presented to students scoring in the top 50 percent in all events.

 Health Fitness Award—awarded to all other participants.

 Participant Physical Fitness Award—presented to students who complete all items but score below the top 50 percent in one or more items.

 Active Lifestyle Award—recognizes students who participate in daily physical activity of any type for five days per week, 60 minutes a day, or 11,000 pedometer steps for six weeks.

The five activities

1. Curl-Ups or Sit-Ups measure abdominal muscle strength.

- Lie on the floor with your arms across your chest and your legs bent. Have a partner hold your feet.

- Lift your upper body off the ground, and then lower it until it just touches the floor.

- Repeat as many times as you can in one minute.

2. Shuttle Run measures leg strength and endurance.

- Run to the blocks and pick one up.

- Bring it back to the starting line.

- Repeat with the other block.

3. One-Mile Run or Walk measures leg muscle strength and heart and lung endurance.

- Run or walk a mile as fast as you can.

4. Pull-Ups measure the strength and endurance of arm and shoulder muscles.

- Hang by your hands from a bar.

- Pull your body up until your chin is over the bar. Lower your body again without touching the floor.

- Repeat as many times as you can.

5. V-Sit Reach measures the flexibility of your legs and back.

- Sit on the floor with your feet behind the line.

- Reach forward as far as you can.

© Harcourt

Being Physically Active
Warm-Up and Cool-Down Stretches

Before you exercise, you should always warm up your muscles. The warm-up stretches shown here should be held for at least fifteen to twenty seconds and repeated at least three times. At the end of your workout, spend about two minutes repeating some of these stretches.

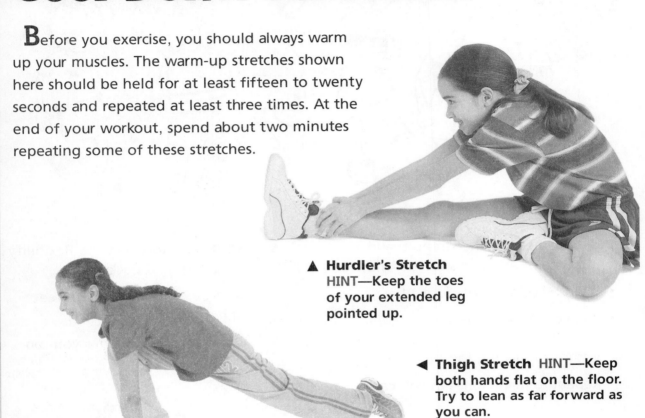

▲ **Hurdler's Stretch** HINT—Keep the toes of your extended leg pointed up.

◄ **Thigh Stretch** HINT—Keep both hands flat on the floor. Try to lean as far forward as you can.

► **Upper-Back and Shoulder Stretch** HINT—Try to stretch your hand down so that it lies flat against your back.

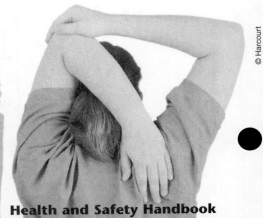

▼ **Sit-and-Reach Stretch**
HINT—Remember to bend at the waist. Keep your eyes on your toes!

▼ **Shoulder and Chest Stretch** HINT—Pulling your hands slowly toward the floor makes this stretch more effective. Keep your elbows straight, but not locked!

▲ **Calf Stretch** HINT—Remember to keep both feet on the floor during this stretch. Try changing the distance between your feet. Is the stretch better for you when your legs are closer together or farther apart?

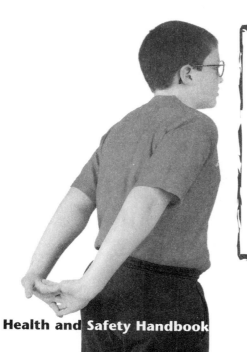

Tips for Stretching

- Never bounce when stretching.

- Remember to hold each stretch for fifteen to twenty seconds.

- Breathe normally. This helps your body get the oxygen it needs.

- Stretch only until you feel a slight pull, NOT until it hurts.

Being Physically Active
Planning Your Weekly Activities

Being active every day is important for your overall health. Physical activity strengthens your body systems and helps you manage stress and maintain a healthful weight. The Activity Pyramid, like the Food Guide Pyramid, can help you make a variety of choices in the right amounts to keep your body strong and healthy.

The Activity Pyramid

Sitting Still
Watching television, playing computer games
Small amounts of time

Light Exercise
Playtime, yardwork, softball
2–3 times a week

Strength and Flexibility Exercises
Weight training, dancing, pull-ups
2–3 times a week

Aerobic Exercises
Biking, running, soccer, hiking
30+ minutes, 2–3 times a week

Routine Activities
Walking to school, taking the stairs, helping with housework
Every day

First Aid
For Bleeding–Universal Precautions

You can get some diseases from a person's blood. Avoid touching anyone's blood. Wear protective gloves if possible. To treat an injury, follow the steps.

If someone else is bleeding

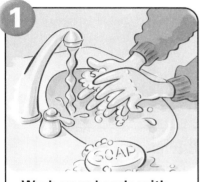

1 Wash your hands with soap if possible.

2 Put on protective gloves, if available.

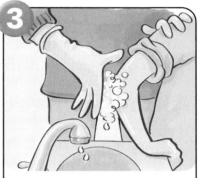

3 Wash small wounds with soap and water. Do not wash serious wounds.

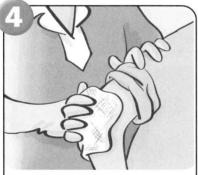

4 Place a clean gauze pad or cloth over the wound. Press firmly for ten minutes. Don't lift the gauze during this time.

5 If you don't have gloves, have the injured person hold the gauze or cloth in place with his or her hand for ten minutes.

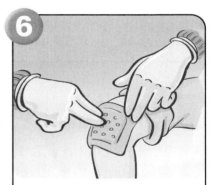

6 If after ten minutes the bleeding has stopped, bandage the wound. If the bleeding has not stopped, continue pressing on the wound and get help.

If you are bleeding

Follow the steps above. You do not need to avoid touching your own blood.

First Aid

For Burns

- Minor burns are called first-degree burns and involve only the top layer of skin. The skin is red and dry, and the burn is painful.

- Second-degree burns cause deeper damage. The burns cause blisters, redness, swelling, and pain.

- Third-degree burns are the most serious because they damage all layers of the skin. The skin is usually white or charred black. The area may feel numb because the nerve endings have been destroyed.

All burns need immediate first aid.

Minor Burns

- Run cool water over the burn or soak it for at least five minutes.

- Cover the burn with a clean, dry bandage.

- Do not put lotion or ointment on the burn.

More Serious Burns

- Cover the burn with a cool, wet bandage or cloth. Do not break any blisters.

- Do not put lotion or ointment on the burn.

- Get help from an adult right away.

For Nosebleeds

- Sit down, and tilt your head forward. Pinch your nostrils together for at least ten minutes.

- You can also put a cloth-covered cold pack on the bridge of your nose.

- If your nose continues to bleed, get help from an adult.

© Harcourt

First Aid
For Choking
If someone else is choking

1

Recognize the Universal Choking Sign—grasping the throat with both hands. This sign means a person is choking and needs help.

2

Stand behind the person, and put your arms around his or her waist. Place your fist above the person's belly button.

3

Grab your fist with your other hand. Pull your hands toward yourself, and give five quick, hard, upward thrusts on the person's stomach.

If you are choking when alone

1 Make a fist, and place it above your belly button. Grab your fist with your other hand. Pull your hands up with a quick, hard thrust.

2 Or keep your hands on your belly, lean your body over the back of a chair or over a counter, and shove your fist in and up.

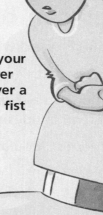

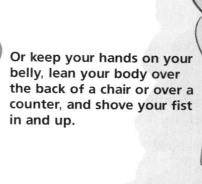

First Aid

For Dental Emergencies

Dental emergencies occur less often than other health emergencies, but it is wise to know how to handle them

Broken Tooth

- Rinse your mouth with warm water. Wrap a cloth around a cold pack, and place it on the injured area. Save any parts of the broken tooth. Call your dentist immediately.

Bitten Tongue or Lip

- Apply direct pressure to the bleeding area with a cloth. Use a wrapped cold pack to stop swelling. If the bleeding doesn't stop within fifteen minutes, go to a hospital emergency room.

Knocked-Out Permanent Tooth

- Find the tooth, and clean it gently and carefully. Handle it by the top (crown), not the root. Put it back into the socket if you can. Hold it in place by biting on a piece of clean cloth. If the tooth cannot be put back in, place it in a cup with milk or water. See a dentist immediately because time is very important in saving the tooth.

Food or Objects Caught Between Teeth

- Use dental floss to gently take out the food or object. Never use anything sharp to remove what is stuck between your teeth. If it cannot be removed, call your dentist.

Remember that many dental injuries can be prevented if you

- wear a mouth guard while playing sports.
- wear a safety belt while riding in a car.
- inspect your home and get rid of hazards that might cause falls and injuries.
- see your dentist regularly for preventive care.

For Insect Bites and Stings

- Always tell an adult about bites and stings.

- Scrape out the stinger with your fingernail.

- Wash the area with soap and water.

- A wrapped ice cube or cold pack will usually take away the pain from insect bites. A paste made from baking soda and water also helps.

- If the bite or sting is more serious and is on an arm or leg, keep the leg or arm dangling down. Apply a cold, wet cloth. Get help immediately!

- If you find a tick on your skin, remove it. Protect your fingers with a tissue or cloth to prevent contact with infectious tick fluids. If you must touch the tick with your bare hands, wash your hands right away.

- If the tick has already bitten you, ask an adult to remove it. Using tweezers, an adult should grab the tick as close to your skin as possible and pull the tick out in one steady motion. Do not use petroleum jelly or oil of any kind because it may cause the tick to struggle, releasing its infectious fluids. Thoroughly wash the area of the bite.

For Skin Rashes from Plants

Many poisonous plants have three leaves. Remember, "Leaves of three, let them be." If you touch a poisonous plant, wash the area and your hands. Change clothes, and wash the ones the plant touched. If a rash develops, follow these tips.

- Apply calamine lotion or a paste of baking soda and water. Try not to scratch. Tell an adult.

- If you get blisters, do not pop them. If they burst, keep the area clean and dry. Cover the area with a bandage.

- If your rash does not go away in two weeks or if the rash is on your face or in your eyes, see your doctor.

Alcohol, Tobacco, and Other Drugs

A Drug-Free School

Schools help their students refuse to use alcohol, tobacco, and other drugs. Many schools make rules and sponsor activities to encourage people to say *no* to drugs.

DRUG-FREE SCHOOL ZONE

MINIMUM 3 YEARS IN PRISON TO SELL, PURCHASE, MANUFACTURE, DELIVER OR POSSESS WITH INTENT TO SELL AN ILLEGAL DRUG WITHIN 1,000 FEET OF A SCHOOL STATE. STATUTE 893

School Rules

Your school probably has rules about drugs. Many schools decide to be drug-free zones. They often have strict penalties for anyone found with drugs. For example, anyone found with drugs may be expelled or suspended. Learn your school's rules regarding use of drugs.

Positive Peer Pressure

Peer pressure can be bad or good. When people the same age encourage each other to make healthful choices, they are using *positive peer pressure*. In a school, students may make posters or hold rallies to encourage other students to choose not to use drugs.

© Harcourt

Health and Safety Handbook

Alcohol, Tobacco, and Other Drugs

What to Do When Others Use Drugs

You should make a commitment not to use alcohol, tobacco, or other drugs. But you may be around other students or adults who make unhealthful choices. Here is what you can do.

Know the Signs

If someone has a problem with drugs, he or she often acts differently. The person may be sad or angry all the time, skip school or work, or forget important events.

Talk to a Trusted Adult

If you are worried about someone's drug use, don't keep it a secret. Talk to a trusted adult. Ask the adult for help. You can also get support from adults to resist pressure to use drugs.

Be Supportive

If a person has decided to stop using drugs, help him or her stop. Suggest healthful activities you can do together. Tell the person you're happy that he or she has stopped using drugs.

Stay Healthy

If you have a choice, leave any place where drugs are being used. If you cannot leave, stay as far away from the drugs as possible.

Where to Get Help

- Hospitals
- Alateen
- Alcoholics Anonymous
- Narcotics Anonymous
- Al-Anon
- Drug treatment centers

Health and Safety
Backpack Safety

Carrying a backpack that is too heavy can injure your back. Carrying one incorrectly also can hurt you.

Safe Use

- Choose a backpack with wide, padded shoulder straps and a padded back.

- Lighten your load. Leave unnecessary items at home.

- Pack heavier items so that they will be closest to your back.

- Always use both shoulder straps to carry the backpack.

- Never wear a backpack while riding a bicycle. The weight makes it harder to stay balanced. Use the bicycle's basket or saddlebags instead.

▲ This is the right way to wear a backpack.

▲ This is the wrong way to carry a backpack

Safe Weight

A full backpack should weigh no more than 10 to 15 percent of your body weight. Less is better. To find 10 percent, divide your body weight by 10. Here are some examples:

Your Weight (pounds)	Maximum Backpack Weight (pounds)
70	7
80	8
90	9

Health and Safety Handbook

Health and Safety

Bike Safety Check

A safe bike should be the right size for you.

- You should be able to rest your heel on the pedal when you sit on your bike with the pedal in the lowest position.

- When you are standing astride your bike with both feet flat on the ground, your body should be 2 inches above the bar that goes from the handlebar to the seat.

A bike should have all the safety equipment shown below. Does *your* bike pass the test?

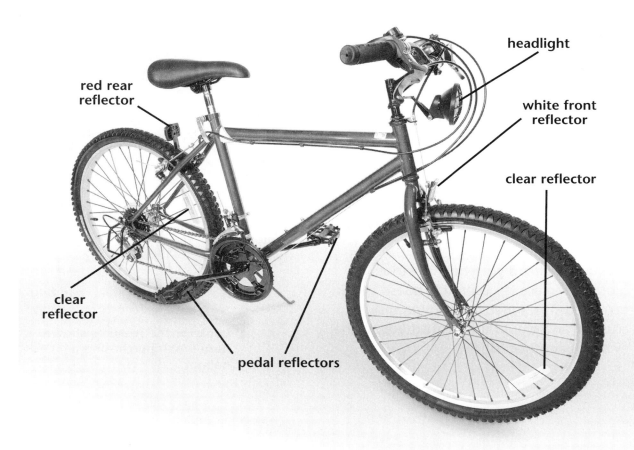

headlight

red rear reflector

white front reflector

clear reflector

clear reflector

pedal reflectors

Safety While Riding

Here are some tips for safe bicycle riding.

- Always wear your bike helmet, even for short distances.

- Check your bike every time you ride it. Is it in safe working condition?

- Ride in single file in the same direction as traffic. Never weave in and out of parked cars.

- Before you enter a street, **Stop**. **Look** left, right, and then left again. **Listen** for any traffic. **Think** before you go.

- Walk your bike across an intersection. **Look** left, right, and then left again. Wait for traffic to pass.

- Obey all traffic signs and signals.

- Do not ride your bike at night without an adult. Be sure to wear light-colored clothing, have reflectors, and use front and rear lights for night riding.

Your Bike Helmet

- About 500,000 children are involved in bike-related crashes every year. That's why it's important to always wear your bike helmet.

- Wear your helmet properly. It should lie flat on your head and be strapped snugly so it will stay in place if you fall.

- If you do fall and your helmet strikes the ground, replace it—even if it doesn't look damaged. The inner foam lining may be crushed and would not protect you in the event of another fall.

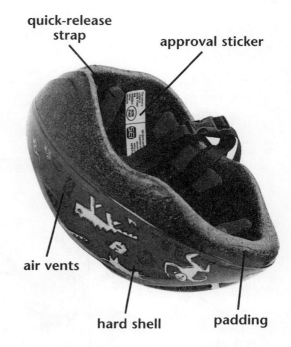

quick-release strap

approval sticker

air vents

hard shell

padding

▲ Look for the features shown here when purchasing a helmet.

© Harcourt

Health and Safety

Summer and Backyard Safety

Use this list to check for hazards before playing in your own or a friend's backyard.

Poison Plants such as poison ivy, poinsettias, certain mushrooms, and oleander are just some of the plants that are poisonous. Use caution around yard chemicals, such as fertilizers, pesticides, pool chemicals, and pet products.

Fire Be careful around barbecue grills, lighter fluid, and bonfires. Fires can get out of hand very quickly, and accidents can happen before anyone realizes what is happening.

Water Do not leave small children unattended near swimming pools, kiddie pools, and large basins. Use a life jacket when boating. Wear boat shoes around wet and slippery decks.

Cutting Tools and Power Tools Treat lawn mowers and all power tools with respect. Never leave them unattended where a child might turn them on.

Strangling Hazards Use caution around fences, decks, and stairway railings. Clotheslines and rope can also be hazardous if a small child gets caught in them. Always use care when playing on or around swings.

Falling Remember to use good sense and good manners around climbing bars, ladders, and tree houses. Pushing or shoving a person can cause cuts, broken bones, and knocked-out teeth.

Insects and Other Animals Remember that ticks, mosquitoes, bees, or other flying insects can cause diseases or bites that can be fatal. Strange dogs wandering into your backyard may be dangerous and should be avoided.

Sun Remember to use sunscreen, wear a hat, and drink plenty of liquids when out in the sun. Sunburn or heatstroke can put a quick or painful end to a fun day.

Health and Safety
Thunderstorm Safety

Thunderstorms are severe storms. Lightning can injure or kill people, cause fires, and damage property. Here are thunderstorm safety tips.

- **If you are inside, stay there.** The safest place to be is inside a building.

- **If you are outside, try to take shelter.** If possible, get into a closed car or truck. If you can't take shelter, get into a ditch or another low area.

- **If you are outside, stay away from tall objects.** Don't stand in an open field, on a beach, on a hilltop, or near a lone tree. Find a low place and crouch down, with only your feet touching the ground.

- **Stay away from water.** Lightning is attracted to water, and water conducts electricity.

- **Listen for weather bulletins.** Storms that produce lightning may also produce tornadoes. Be ready to take shelter in a basement or in a hallway or other room without windows.

Earthquake Safety

An earthquake is a strong shaking of the ground. The tips below, many for adults, can help you and your family stay safe.

Before an Earthquake	During an Earthquake	After an Earthquake
• Bolt tall, heavy furniture, such as bookcases, to the wall. Store the heaviest items on the lowest shelves.	• If you are outdoors, stay there. Move away from buildings and electric wires.	• Continue to watch for falling objects as aftershocks shake the area.
• To prevent fires, bolt down gas appliances and use flexible hose and connections for both gas and water lines.	• If you are indoors, stay under heavy furniture or in a doorway. Stay away from glass doors and windows and heavy objects that might fall.	• Have the building checked for hidden structural problems.
• Firmly anchor overhead light fixtures to the ceiling to keep them from falling.	• If you are in a car, go to an open area away from buildings and overpasses.	• Check for broken gas, electric, and water lines. If you smell gas, shut off the gas main and leave the area. Report the leak.

© Harcourt

Blizzard Safety

A blizzard is a dangerous snowstorm with strong winds and heavy snowfall. It may last for 12 to 36 hours, with snowfall greater than 6 inches in 24 hours and winds gusting higher than 35 miles per hour. Visibility may be less than $\frac{1}{4}$ mile. The following tips can help you and your family stay safe during a blizzard.

Your home should have

- a working flashlight with extra batteries.
- a battery-powered NOAA weather radio, radio, or TV.
- extra food and water, plus medicines and baby items if needed.
- first-aid supplies.
- heating fuel such as propane, kerosene, or fuel oil.
- an emergency heating source.
- a smoke detector and a fire extinguisher.

If traveling by car or truck, your family should

- keep the gas tank nearly full. The vehicle should be fully checked and properly prepared for winter use.
- always let a friend or relative know the family's travel plans.
- keep a blizzard survival kit in the vehicle. It should contain blankets; a flashlight with extra batteries; a can and waterproof matches to melt snow for drinking; and high-calorie, nonperishable food.
- remain in the vehicle in a blizzard, and tie something bright to the antenna. Run the motor for short times for heat. Use the inside light only while running the motor.

Health and Safety

Evaluating Health Websites

Many people find health facts on the Web. The Web is a valuable information resource. However, it's important to remember that almost anyone can put information on the Web. You need to learn how to tell good, reliable websites from bad, unreliable ones. Here are some questions to think about when you are looking at health websites.

Who controls the website?

A site can be biased, or slanted, toward one viewpoint. Look for sources that you know. Sites run by a university (.edu) or by the government (.gov) are usually more reliable. A site run by one person whom you've never heard of is probably less reliable.

Who is saying it?

Information from doctors, nurses, and health professionals is usually reliable. Look for the initials of a college degree after the writer's name—*M.D., R.N., Ph.D., Pharm.D.,* and so on. Reputable newspaper and magazine sites usually check their facts with a health professional, so, they're usually reliable as well.

© Harcourt

Does the site look good?

Frequent spelling or grammar mistakes and poor design are warning signs. If the site didn't take time to fix simple mistakes, perhaps it didn't take the time to check the facts, either.

Are they selling something?

Sites that are trying to sell a product may not be reliable. Often, they tell you only what makes their products or services look good. Nonprofit sites are usually more reliable.

What is the evidence?

Personal stories sound convincing. However, they are not as reliable as scientifically tested information. Look for sites with evidence from science research.

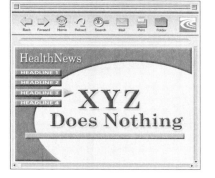

Does everyone agree?

Always try to check more than one source. If several sites agree on the facts, they are probably reliable.

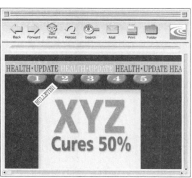

Health and Safety

Good Posture at the Computer

Good posture is very important when using the computer. To help prevent eyestrain, muscle fatigue, and injuries, follow the posture tips shown below. Remember to grasp your mouse lightly, keep your back straight, avoid facing your monitor toward a window, and take frequent breaks for stretching.

top of screen at or just below eye level

shoulders in line with ears and hips

neck and shoulders relaxed

arms at sides, bent as shown

wrists straight

feet flat on floor

Safety on the Internet

The Internet is a remarkable tool. You can use it for fun, education, research, and more. However, like anything else, it has some downsides. Some people compare the Internet to a city—not all the people there are people you want to meet, and not all the places you can go are places you want to be. On the Internet, as in a real city, you have to use common sense and follow safety guidelines to protect yourself. Below are some easy rules you can follow to stay safe online.

Rules for Online Safety

- Talk with an adult family member to set up rules for going online. Decide when you can go online, how long you can be online, and what kinds of places you can visit. Do not break the rules you agree to follow.

- Don't give out personal information such as your name, address, and telephone number or information about your family. Don't give the name or location of your school.

- If you find anything online that makes you uncomfortable, tell an adult family member right away.

- Never agree to meet with anyone in person. If you want to get together with someone you have met online, check with an adult family member first. If a meeting is approved, arrange to meet in a public place, and bring an adult with you.

- Don't send your picture or anything else to a person you meet online without first checking with an adult.

- Don't respond to any messages that are mean or make you uncomfortable. If you receive a message like that, tell an adult right away.

Health and Safety
Family Emergency Plan

By having a plan, your family can protect itself during an emergency. To make an emergency plan, your family needs to gather information, make some choices, and practice parts of the plan.

Know What Could Happen

Learn the possible emergencies that might happen in your area. Fires and storms can happen almost anywhere. You may also be at risk for earthquakes or floods. List the possible emergencies.

Have Two Meeting Places

Pick two places to meet, one near your home and one farther away. The first place should be only far enough away to be safe in case of a fire. For example, you could meet at the corner of your block. The second place could be the main door to your school, a relative's house, or where a family member works.

Know Your Family Contact

Choose someone who lives far away to be a contact person. This person will help your family stay in touch. If a family member becomes lost during an emergency, he or she can call the contact person. Each family member should memorize the full name, address, and telephone number of the contact.

Out-of-State Contact

Ms. Jane Doe
43212 Janeway Blvd.
Big City, IL 12345
(123) 555-1234

Practice Evacuating

During a fire, you need to evacuate, or get out of, your home right away. Look at your list of possible emergencies. Use it to help you plan how to evacuate each room of your home. Practice evacuating at least twice a year.

▼ This woman is showing her daughter how to turn off the main water valve at their home.

Learn How to Turn Off Utilities

Water, electricity, and gas are *utilities*. An emergency may damage utility pipes or wires and make them dangerous. This can damage or even destroy a home. With an adult's help, learn when and how to turn off utilities. If tools are needed to turn off a utility, those tools should be stored close by. **CAUTION:** If you turn off the gas, a professional must turn it back on.

▲ outdoor water shut-off valve

Make an Emergency Supply Kit

After an emergency, your family may need food, blankets, clean water to drink, and first-aid supplies. The American Red Cross or other emergency organizations can give your family a checklist for making an emergency supply kit.

© Harcourt

1. STOP

Fire Safety

Fires cause more deaths than any other type of disaster. But a fire doesn't have to be deadly if you and your family prepare your home and follow some basic safety rules.

- Install smoke detectors outside sleeping areas and on any additional floors of your home. Be sure to test the smoke detectors once a month and change the batteries in each detector twice a year.

- Keep a fire extinguisher on each floor of your home. Check monthly to make sure each is properly charged.

- Make a family emergency plan. See page 118 for help. Ideally, there should be two routes out of each room. Sleeping areas are most important, because most fires happen at night. Plan to use stairs only; elevators can be dangerous in a fire.

- Designate one person to call the fire department or 911 from a neighbor's home.

- Practice crawling low to avoid smoke. If your clothes catch fire, follow the three steps shown.

2. DROP

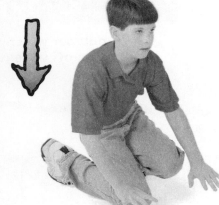

3. ROLL

© Harcourt

Health and Safety
Caring for Your Skin

- Your skin is a complicated organ that protects you from diseases and helps keep your body from drying out.

- A daily bath or shower helps remove dirt, germs, dead skin cells, and excess oil from your skin.

- Because of all the changes that occur during puberty, it is very important to practice good hygiene to control body odor.

▲ **Using products such as these will keep your skin clean and healthy.**

- The sun can be more damaging for your skin than dirt and germs. Too much sun can make your skin become wrinkled, tough, and leathery. It can also cause skin cancer, which can lead to death.

- Covering up with clothing and wearing a hat give you good protection from the sun. Protect uncovered skin with sunscreen, even on cloudy days.

▲ **Using sunscreen even on cloudy days will protect your skin from the sun's harmful rays.**

Health and Safety
Safety near Water

Water can be very dangerous—a person can drown in five minutes or less. The best way to be safer near water is to learn how to swim. You should also follow these rules:

- Never swim without a lifeguard or a responsible adult present.

- If you can't swim, stay in shallow water. Don't rely on an inflatable raft.

- Know the rules for the beach or pool, and obey them. Don't run or play roughly near water.

- Do not dive in head-first until you know the water is deep enough. Jump in feet-first the first time.

- Watch the weather. Get out of the water at once if you see lightning or hear thunder.

- Protect your skin with sunscreen and your eyes with sunglasses.

- Wear a Coast Guard-approved life jacket anytime you are in a boat.

- Know what to do in an emergency.

Health and Safety
Safety near Motor Vehicles

Cars and trucks are large, dangerous machines. Always be careful when you are in and around them.

As a Pedestrian

Anytime you are walking near traffic or moving vehicles, you should follow these safety rules:

- If you have to walk on roads where there is no sidewalk, walk facing oncoming traffic. Stay out of the middle of the road. Avoid walking on roads after sunset.

- Be alert for vehicles that are backing up or turning.

- Be sure that drivers can see you clearly at all times.

As a Passenger

What you do as a passenger affects your safety. It can also affect the safety of everyone in the car. You should follow these safety rules:

- Always wear a safety belt. If there isn't a safety belt for everyone, don't ride in that car.

- Never ride in the cargo area of a station wagon, pickup truck, hatchback, or van.

- Keep sharp or heavy objects in the trunk.

- Stay seated and face forward.

- Don't distract the driver. Don't throw objects or make sudden, loud noises. Don't tease or behave disruptively. Keep your hands, feet, body, and objects to yourself.

- Follow the driver's instructions at all times.

- Ride only with good drivers who have well-maintained vehicles. Never ride with strangers.

- Never ride with a driver who has been drinking alcohol or using drugs.

▶ Always wear a safety belt.

Health and Safety

Safety Tips for Babysitters

Being a babysitter is a very important job. As a sitter you are responsible for the safety of the children in your care. Adults depend on you to make good decisions. Here are some tips to help you be a successful and safe babysitter.

When you accept a job as a babysitter, ask

- what time you should arrive.

- how long the adults will be away.

- what your responsibilities will be.

- the amount of pay you will receive.

- what arrangements will be made for your transportation to and from the home.

When you arrive to start a job, you should

- arrive several minutes early so that the adults have time to give you information about caring for the child.

- write down the name and phone number of the place the adults are going and what time they will be home.

- find out where emergency phone numbers are listed. The list should have numbers for the police, the fire department, and the children's doctor.

- find out where first-aid supplies are kept. You should be prepared to give first aid in an emergency.

- ask what and when the children should eat.

- ask what activities the children may do.

- ask when the children should go to bed and what their bedtime routine is.

© Harcourt

While you are caring for children, you should

- never leave a baby alone on a changing table, sofa, or bed.

- never leave a child alone, even for a short time.

- check children often when they are sleeping.

- never leave a child alone near a pool or in the bathtub.

- never let a child play with a plastic bag.

- keep dangerous items out of a child's reach.

- know where all the doors are, and keep them locked. Do not let anyone in without permission from the adults.

- take a message if the phone rings. Do not tell the caller that you are the babysitter or that the adults are out.

- call the adults if there is an injury or illness. If you can't reach them, call the emergency numbers on the list.

▲ **Never leave children playing alone.**

▲ **Never leave a child to eat alone.**

◄ **Never leave children alone near a pool or in the bathtub.**

© Harcourt

When Home Alone

Everyone stays home alone sometimes. When you stay home alone, it's important to know how to take care of yourself. Here are some easy rules to follow that will help keep you safe when you are home by yourself.

Do These Things

- Lock all the doors and windows. Be sure you know how to lock and unlock all the locks.

- If someone who is nasty or mean calls, say nothing and hang up immediately. Tell an adult about the call when he or she gets home. Your parents may not want you to answer the phone at all.

- If you have an emergency, call 911. Be prepared to describe the problem and to give your full name, address, and telephone number. Follow all instructions given to you. Do not hang up the phone until you are told to do so.

- If you see anyone hanging around outside your home, call a neighbor or the police.

- If you see or smell smoke, go outside right away. If you live in an apartment, do not take the elevator. Go to a neighbor's house, and call 911 immediately.

- Entertain yourself. Time will pass more quickly if you are not bored. Work on a hobby, read a book or magazine, do your homework, or clean your room. Before you know it, an adult will be home.

© Harcourt

Do Not Do These Things

- Do NOT use the stove, microwave, or oven unless an adult family member has given you permission and you know how to use these appliances.

- Do NOT open the door to anyone you don't know or to anyone who is not supposed to be in your home.

- Do NOT talk to strangers on the telephone. Do not tell anyone that you are home alone. If the call is for an adult family member, say that he or she can't come to the phone right now and take a message.

- Do NOT have friends over unless an adult family member has given you permission to do so.

▶ A caller ID display can help you decide whether to answer the phone.

© Harcourt

Activity Book Answer Key • Chapter 1

Growth and Development

Quick Study
Pages 1–2

Lesson 1
Summary: respiratory system, circulatory system, excretory system
Lesson Details:
skeletal
respiratory
move food through the digestive tract
cause muscles to move

Lesson 2
Summary: sperm, embryo, fetus, genes, DNA
Lesson Details:
3, 2, 4
6, 1, 5

Lesson 3
Summary: pituitary gland, endocrine system, puberty, adolescence
Lesson Details: testes: testosterone, sperm; ovaries: eggs, estrogen

Lesson 4
Summary: maturity
Lesson Details: Possible answers: want to be more independent, but want support and understanding; want privacy and time alone

Lesson 5
Summary: abstinence
Lesson Details: Answers will vary. Check answers for appropriateness.

Reading Skill
Page 3

Answer to question: Blood carried by the artery from the heart to the lungs is oxygen-poor. Blood carried by the veins from the lungs to the heart is oxygen-rich.

The blood flows through the vena cava from the body to the right atrium and then into the right ventricle. Blood from the right ventricle flows to the lungs to be rid of wastes and pick up oxygen. Blood from the lungs flows to the left atrium and then into the left ventricle. From there it flows to the body through the aorta.

Problem Solving
Page 4

A. Possible answer: Andy started with "I," but the rest of his statement was a "you" message that accused Davis. He could say, "I'm sorry I said those things. I want us to be friends." Then he could use "I" messages to explain why he doesn't want to be called a nickname. He can listen to Davis and gather feedback about how the friendship is working.

B. Possible answer: Juanita could use "I" messages to tell her parents why she thinks she is mature enough to baby-sit. If her parents say no, she could offer to take a baby-sitting course at a local college or hospital. She could take care of her brother while her parents are home. Juanita could then ask for feedback after she has taken care of her brother.

Vocabulary Reinforcement
Page 5

1. nervous system
2. embryo
3. skeletal system
4. pituitary gland
5. heredity
6. correct
7. hormones
8. nucleus
9. correct
10. correct

Personal and Consumer Health

Quick Study
Pages 6–7

Lesson 1

Summary: acne, sunscreen
Lesson Details: Possible answer: Acne forms when oil from the oil glands in the dermis plugs the skin's pores. Acne bacteria in the plugged pores cause pimples to form.

Lesson 2

Summary: consumers, advertising, ingredients
Lesson Details: Ads will vary.

Lesson 3

Summary: plaque, floss
Lesson Details: Plaque builds up on the surface of teeth. ➡ Bacteria in plaque act on sugars in foods, forming acids. ➡ Acids cause cavities to form in the tooth's enamel.

Lesson 4

Summary: sties, conjunctivitis, decibels
Lesson Details: Possible answers: Wash your hands before touching your eyes; never look directly at the sun; never put anything into your ear, avoid loud sounds.

Lesson 5

Summary: distraction, repetitive strain injuries
Lesson Details: Head/Shoulders—relaxed, shoulders aligned with ears and hips. Eyes—top of screen just below eye level; screen placed to avoid a glare. Arms/Hands—at your sides, bent at a 90° angle; wrists straight; learn to type correctly. Legs/Feet—sit with thighs horizontal to the floor, feet flat on floor.

Lesson 6

Summary: reliable

Lesson Details: Possible answers: dentist, dental hygienist, ADA website

Reading Skill
Page 8
Details: What I read: The cochlea changes sound vibrations into electrical signals the brain interprets as sound; the hair cells within the cochlea can be damaged by strong vibrations, caused by loud sounds. Damage to the cells in the cochlea can cause hearing loss. **What I know:** Answers will vary.
Conclusion: It is important to protect your ears from loud noises.

Problem Solving
Page 9

A. Possible answer: The most trustworthy and responsible decision Henry can make would be to talk to a parent or his doctor before using the product Miguel uses.

B. Possible answer: Her decision is not responsible because her dentist told her to brush after each meal. She could ask another girl with braces to brush her teeth at the same time Niomi does at school. She could ask if she could brush her teeth in the nurse's office after lunch.

Vocabulary Reinforcement
Page 10

1. the top layer of skin
2. a product that helps protect skin from the sun's harmful rays
3. the process of giving people information and ideas that encourage them to buy something
4. a substance that coats teeth and leads to tooth decay
5. a sight condition in which distant objects appear blurry
6. units used to measure the loudness of sound
7. injuries that result from making the same motions over and over again
8. something that takes one's attention away

Activity Book Answer Key • Chapter 3

Preparing Healthful Foods

Quick Study
Pages 11–12

Lesson 1

Summary: carbohydrates, fats, proteins, calories, minerals, Vitamins, fiber, Cholesterol

Lesson Details: Possible answer: Different vitamins are found in different foods. You have to eat a variety of foods in order to get all of the vitamins you need.

Lesson 2

Summary: balanced diet, Food Guide Pyramid, serving, vegetarian

Lesson Details: 3, 2–4, 6–9

Lesson 3

Summary: staple

Lesson Details:

	vegetable oil	chilies, onion, lettuce, tomato, olives
tofu		carrots, red pepper, zucchini
beef, chicken, lamb	olive oil	

Lesson 4

Summary: anorexia, bulimia, nutritional deficiency

Lesson Details: Aim for Fitness, Build a Healthy Base, Choose Sensibly

Lesson 5

Summary: convenience foods, Additives, preservatives

Lesson Details: The maximum amount of fat in one serving is 3 grams.

Reading Skill
Page 13

Possible answers:

Alike

nutrients needed by the body

same amount of energy per gram

Different

Proteins are used to build the body and for growth.

Carbohydrates are used for energy.

Carbohydrates are found in fruits, vegetables, and grains.

Proteins are found in meats, poultry, fish, dried beans, eggs, and nuts.

Problem Solving
Page 14

A. Keyona's menu choice was not the most healthful and responsible choice. Possible explanation: A cheeseburger and french fries have more fat than other choices on the menu. A more healthful decision would have been to order the baked chicken with baked potato.

B. Possible answer: Lee should choose fruit, such as an apple or a banana. Fruits give quick energy and are healthful choices. This snack will help Lee follow his family's rules because it is healthful. Although candy and sweets give quick energy, they are not healthful choices.

Vocabulary Reinforcement
Page 15

1. k	7. f
2. b	8. a
3. l	9. g
4. e	10. h
5. c	11. i
6. j	12. d

Activity Book Answer Key • Chapter 4

Keeping Active

Quick Study
Pages 16–17

Lesson 1

Summary: muscular strength, muscular endurance, flexibility, cardiovascular fitness
Lesson Details: 365 (215 + 150), 400, 270

Lesson 2

Summary: workout, warm-up, cool-down, Aerobic exercise, target heart rate, Anaerobic exercise
Lesson Details: Possible answer: Sleep will help you feel alert and give you energy for physical activities.

Lesson 3

Summary: hyperthermia, hypothermia
Lesson Details: mouth guards; helmets; special pads or guards for knees, elbows, shins, and wrists; protective glasses or goggles

Reading Skills
Page 18

Answers may vary slightly.

A. Possible answers:
1. You consume more calories than your body uses. You gain weight.
2. You build and maintain strong bones, muscles, and joints. You control your weight. You prevent high blood pressure. You reduce stress. You boost self-esteem. You think more clearly.

B. regular aerobic exercise
C. You could drown or be injured.
D. You might injure your neck, back, or shoulders.

Problem Solving
Page 19

Answers will vary.

A. Possible answer: Jeremy could set a goal to lose weight by consuming fewer calories than he uses each day. He could plan to eat smaller portions of food, eliminate unhealthful snacks, and exercise an additional day each week. He could monitor his progress by recording his weight. He could then evaluate his progress after a month or so, making necessary adjustments if he has not reached his goal. If he achieves his goal, he could set a new goal to maintain his weight.

B. Possible answer: She could set a goal to increase her muscular endurance and cardiovascular fitness. Her plan might include running, swimming, or fast walking for at least 20 minutes three times a week. She could monitor her progress by recording the time it takes to cover a specific distance. She could evaluate her progress during practice matches with a friend.

Vocabulary Reinforcement
Page 20

A. 1. i
2. a
3. d
4. e
5. b
6. h
7. j
8. g
9. c
10. f

B. Check students' paragraphs.

Activity Book Answer Key • Chapter 5

Staying Safe Every Day

Quick Study
Pages 21–22

Lesson 1

Summary: electric shock, flammable, fire hazard

Lesson Details: Answers should reflect kitchen safety tips listed on pages 150–151.

Lesson 2

Summary: weapon, poison

Lesson Details: Students' answers will vary but should reflect responsible behavior and the safety measures listed on page 154 of the textbook.

Lesson 3

Summary: reach and throw, survival floating

Lesson Details: Box 1: Rest—Lie on the surface of the water with head, arms, and legs in the water. Box 2: Surface—Raise arms and move legs properly when you need to breathe. Box 3: Breathe—Push down with arms, bring legs together, bring nose and mouth out of the water, and breathe. Box 4: Sink—Hold your breath, and let your body return to resting position.

Lesson 4

Summary: gang, terrorism

Lesson Details: Possible answers: discourage him from joining the gang, help him find community or school groups that can help him feel safe, encourage him to talk with a parent or other trusted adult

Reading Skill
Page 23

Main Idea: Warning signs can show dangerous electrical situations inside and outside the home.

Indoor Details: Damaged electrical cord coatings; Water near electrical appliances; Overloaded outlets or missing outlet covers

Outdoor Details: Downed electrical wires; Damaged or dangerous lines; Trees with branches near power lines

Problem Solving
Page 24

A. Students' answers will vary but should reflect the steps to resolve conflicts and result in a solution that will allow Eddie and Samantha to remain responsible and trustworthy teammates.

B. Students' answers will vary but should follow the steps to resolve conflicts and result in a solution that shows respect and trustworthiness.

Vocabulary Reinforcement
Page 25

1. poison
2. gang
3. flammable
4. terrorism
5. fire hazard
6. survival floating
7. weapon
8. electric shock
9. reach and throw

© Harcourt

Activity Book Answer Key • Chapter 6

Emergencies and First Aid

Quick Study
Pages 26–27

Lesson 1

Summary: disaster, supply kit

Lesson Details: (1) Create an escape plan. (2) Dress warmly in thin layers. (3) See p. 182 for possible answers. (4) Stay away from windows. (5) Move valuables to a higher level. (6) See p. 183 for possible answers.

Lesson 2

Summary: first aid, fracture, sprain, seizure, hyperthermia, hypothermia, frostbite

Lesson Details: Rest helps reduce bleeding, prevents further injury, and speeds healing. Ice limits swelling and pain. Apply an ice pack or cold pack for twenty minutes every two to three hours for one to two days. Compress the injured area by wrapping it with an elastic bandage for about two days. Loosen the bandage if it gets too tight. Elevate the injured area, or keep it above the heart level, several times a day for one to two days. This will reduce swelling and bleeding. The RICE treatment is appropriate for minor sprains and most minor sports injuries.

Lesson 3

Summary: abdominal thrusts, Rescue breathing, shock

Lesson Details: Choking

Unconsciousness or does not respond; no sign of breathing can be heard or felt

Apply direct pressure on wound and elevate it above the level of the heart.

Restlessness; shallow breathing; moist, clammy skin.

Determine information about the person and the substance that was swallowed. Call Poison Control Center.

Reading Skill
Page 28

Possible answer: They prepared an escape plan in case of fire. They had smoke alarms in their home. Teri and her sister and brother used a window rather than going downstairs, where the smoke was dense. The family met outside on the sidewalk, as they had discussed. After they briefly huddled together, Teri's mother ran to a neighbor's house to call for emergency help.

Problem Solving
Page 29

A. Possible answer: Sean should give the location of the accident, describe the nature of the accident, and identify how many people might need help. He should then listen carefully to questions the operator may ask and should follow the directions of the operator.

B. Possible answer: After talking with the mother, Trish should call the doctor to explain the situation and listen carefully for the doctor's instructions. She should follow the doctor's instructions and be prepared to tell the mother everything that the doctor said. She should describe what she did to help the child.

Vocabulary Reinforcement
Page 30

A. 1. hypothermia
   2. abdominal thrusts
   3. first aid
   4. disaster
   5. frostbite
   6. hyperthermia
   7. shock
   8. sprain

B. Check students' sentences.

Activity Book Answer Key • Chapter 7

Controlling Disease

Quick Study
Pages 31–32

Lesson 1

Summary: health risk factor, pathogen

Lesson Details: Possible answers:

1. inherited traits that increase your chances of becoming ill
2. harmful conditions in the environment that increase your chances of becoming ill
3. harmful behaviors that increase your chances of becoming ill

Lesson 2

Summary: communicable disease, sexually transmitted diseases (STDs), abstinence, infection, toxins

Lesson Details:

Viruses   smallpox, chicken pox, mumps
Bacteria   strep throat, food poisoning, syphilis
Fungi   athlete's foot
Protozoa   malaria

Lesson 3

Summary: resistance, immune system, antibodies, immunity, immunization, vaccine, Boosters, antibiotic

Lesson Details: Possible answers:

fever—slows the growth of some bacteria; skin— blocks pathogens from entering the body; mucus membranes—trap pathogens as they enter the body

Lesson 4

Summary: Noncommunicable diseases, cardiovascular disease, carcinogens, insulin

Lesson Details: Possible answer: Carcinogens are substances that cause cancer.

Lesson 5

Summary: Stress

Lesson Details: Possible answers:

1. Exercise vigorously.   2. Take time to relax.
3. Talk to someone about your feelings.

Reading Skill
Page 33

Alike

Both increase the risk of disease.

Different

have no control over hereditary risk factors

have control over behavioral risk factors

an example of a disease affected by hereditary risk factors: heart disease; an example of a behavioral risk factor: smoking

Problem Solving
Page 34

A. Possible answer: Tara should realize the source of her stress. She should talk to her parents or her math teacher about her stress. They may suggest ways to study or reassure her about the test. She should also find a positive way to deal with stress, such as by exercising.

B. Possible answer: Juan should talk to a parent or another trusted adult about his situation. He should do something to relieve his stress, such as exercising. He should feel good about his decision to avoid smoking.

Vocabulary Reinforcement
Page 35

1. communicable diseases
2. toxins
3. antibodies
4. insulin
5. sexually transmitted diseases
6. environmental risk factor
7. pathogens
8. boosters
9. symptom
10. abstinence
11. immunity
12. immunization
13. cardiovascular disease

Activity Book Answer Key • Chapter 8

Drugs and Health

Quick Study
Pages 36–37

Lesson 1
Summary: drug; prescription medicines; over-the-counter medicines

Lesson Details: Possible answer: Prescription medicines must be ordered by a doctor. Over-the-counter medicines can be purchased from store shelves. Prescription medicines and over-the-counter medicines both contain drugs.

Lesson 2
Summary: Drug abuse; dependence; tolerance

Lesson Details:

not eating, sleeping very little, unable to say *no*

chills, fever, nausea, depression, severe pain

severe physical reaction or death

Lesson 3
Summary: Stimulants; depressants; Steroids

Lesson Details: Answers will vary.

Depressants: sleepiness; disrupt brain's messages; slow the heart

Stimulants: muscle twitching; blurred vision; fast, shallow breathing

Lesson 4
Summary: Marijuana; Inhalants

Lesson Details: Answers will vary.

Brain: short-term memory loss; destroys brain cells

Heart: increased heart rate; can cause heart attack

Muscles: interferes with how muscles work; weakens muscles

Lesson 5
Summary: Refuse

Lesson Details: Check students' strategies.

Reading Skill
page 38

Main Idea:
- LSD is a hallucinogenic drug which has immediate and long-term effects on the user.

Details:
- LSD comes in different forms.
- Immediate effects of taking LSD include physical changes and emotional changes.
- Flashbacks can occur after long periods of not taking LSD.

Summary:
- LSD is a hallucinogenic drug that comes in different forms. The immediate effects of taking LSD include physical and emotional changes. Long-term effects include flashbacks.

Problem Solving
Page 39

A. Possible answers: Tessa and Lisa can say *no* to the boys and tell them why they refuse to smoke marijuana. They can tell them it can cause short-term memory loss, lower body temperature, decreased reaction time, and a weakened immune system, along with other side effects.

B. Possible answers: Max can ignore Marcus's suggestion and change the topic of conversation to something else. In the future, Max can choose to spend his time with people who don't make harmful decisions.

Vocabulary Reinforcement
Page 40

A.
1. c	**5.** e
2. d	**6.** b
3. f	**7.** a
4. h	**8.** g

B. Check students' sentences.

Activity Book Answer Key • Chapter 9

Tobacco and Alcohol

Quick Study

Pages 41–42

Lesson 1

Summary: tobacco; nicotine; carbon monoxide; tars

Lesson Details: Possible answers are given. **skin:** wrinkles and sagging skin; **mouth:** risk of mouth cancer; **lungs:** breathing is difficult; risk developing emphysema; **brain:** dependence on nicotine develops; **throat:** makes voice gravelly; risk of throat and larynx cancer; **heart:** risk of developing heart disease

Lesson 2

Summary: environmental tobacco smoke (ETS); smokeless tobacco

Lesson Details: Possible answers: Using smokeless tobacco can cause sores in the mouth and throat that can become cancerous; one usage of smokeless tobacco has as much nicotine as two cigarettes; smokeless tobacco can cause a person to lose his or her teeth.

Lesson 3

Summary: blood alcohol level; intoxicated; Alcoholism; alcoholic

Lesson Details: dizziness; loss of balance; behavior changes that may lead to violence

Lesson 4

Summary: negative peer pressure; self-respect

Lesson Details: Possible answers: Advertisers want young people to start drinking and smoking because the sooner they start, the more likely they are to become addicted to these products. The advertising is inaccurate because it shows smokers and drinkers as attractive, energetic, and successful, but the ads do not show how tobacco and alcohol use eventually damages the body.

Lesson 5

Summary: Alcohol-abuse counselors; Recovery programs

Lesson Details: Possible answers: miss a lot of school or work; altered moods including anger; smell like alcohol

Reading Skill

Page 43

Effect:

Tobacco use by smokers: Increased risk of mouth, throat, larynx, esophageal, and lung cancers; Half (50 percent) of people who continue to use tobacco after being diagnosed with emphysema and certain types of cancer die of tobacco-related diseases.

Tobacco use by pregnant women: Babies are born prematurely or have a low birth weight. **Tobacco use around children:** Children develop asthma and have more illnesses.

Problem Solving

Page 44

A. Possible answers: James can say *no* because Dylan's mother will notice that the cigarettes have been opened. Also, when James gets home, his own parents will smell smoke on him. Finally, James can suggest that they do something else instead. If Dylan doesn't agree, James should leave the situation.

B. Possible answers: Tia can change the subject by saying, "No thanks; can you help me decide which skirt to wear to the party?" Tia can say *no* and explain that she does not like feeling dizzy. Or she can tell Sara it's not cool to do something that might make her sick.

Vocabulary Reinforcement

Page 45

A. **Across**
   1. tobacco
   2. carbon monoxide
   7. smokeless tobacco
   8. BAL
   9. intoxicated

   Down
   1. tar
   3. alcoholism
   4. nicotine
   5. alcoholic
   6. ETS

B. Check students' sentences.

Activity Book Answer Key • Chapter 10

Setting Goals

Quick Study
Pages 46–47

Lesson 1

Summary: self-concept, self-respect, body image

Lesson Details:

How you would like other people to think of you

How you think other people think of you

How you think of yourself

How well you understand your feelings and ideas

Lesson 2

Summary: goal

Lesson Details: Check students' goals and plans.

Lesson 3

Summary: aggression, self-control, stress, relaxation

Lesson Details:

aggression forceful words and feelings expressed without self-control

stress butterflies in your stomach, sweaty palms

anxiety trouble eating or sleeping, poor concentration, headaches

Lesson 4

Summary: peers, peer pressure

Lesson Details: Possible answer: Negative and positive peer pressure are both forms of pressure from your peers. Negative peer pressure tries to get you to do things that are illegal or harmful. Positive peer pressure leads you to take part in healthful, safe activities.

Lesson 5

Summary: stereotype, prejudice

Lesson Details: Possible answer: Stereotypes and prejudice can lead people to believe things that are not true about a group of people. These negative feelings can prevent people from working together, since they assume bad things about the group.

Lesson 6

Summary: conflict, conflict resolution

Lesson Details: Check students' responses.

Reading Skill
Page 48

Main Idea: Conflicts are a stressful part of life, but they can be resolved in a peaceful way.

Detail: In a conflict, you must express your ideas clearly and listen as others express their ideas.

Detail: Brainstorming can be used to develop a list of possible resolutions to the conflict.

Detail: A choice has to be made to resolve the conflict. It will probably not please everybody completely.

Problem Solving
Page 49

A. Possible answer: Ling could realize that she is forgetting because she is nervous about the performance. To deal with her stress, she could take out her script and practice her lines so that they are fresh in her mind. Then she could relax before the performance by listening to some music or taking a walk.

B. Possible answers: Paco should recognize that his sweaty palms and the feeling of butterflies in his stomach are signs of stress caused by his concern about the social studies test. To relieve his stress, Paco can review the information he studied for the test or listen to some music.

Vocabulary Reinforcement
Page 50

A. 1. f   6. b

    2. c   7. d

    3. i   8. e

    4. g   9. h

    5. a   10. j

B. Check students' work.

Activity Book Answer Key • Chapter 11

Family and Responsibility

Quick Study
Pages 51–52

Lesson 1

Summary: responsible, respect, self-discipline
Lesson Details:
~~forgets to take out the trash~~
(calls when she is going to be late)
(does extra chores when needed)
~~whines to get out of family night~~
~~is rude to siblings~~
(tries to work out problems)
~~does whatever he wants to do~~
~~talks back~~
(goes on family outings)
(remembers special days)

Lesson 2

Summary: communication, cooperation, compromise
Lesson Details: Sample answer:
Talk over problems.
Listen closely to other people.
Accept responsibility for your actions.
Admit your mistakes.
Be willing to compromise.

Lesson 3

Summary: sibling
Lesson Details: Possible answers: parents; counselor; clergy; trusted family friend; older sibling; or other adult family member, such as an aunt, an uncle, or a grandparent.

Reading Skill
Page 53

1. Possible answer: Heather thinks Haley is depressed about the family's move.
2. Possible answer: Haley thinks Heather is ignoring her and leaving her out.

3. Possible answer:
   What I read:
   Haley is not adjusting well to her new school. Haley is staying in her room a lot of the time.
   What I know:
   I know that Haley feels left out of Heather's activities. They are twins, and they probably have done a lot together up to now.
   Conclusion:
   Haley needs to get involved in school activities and make some friends. Heather could make an effort to include Haley in her activities with her new friends.

Problem Solving
Page 54

Possible answer: Soledad is happy to finally have her own room. She wants her privacy. She does not want Maria to hang out in her room. Maria probably misses being in the same room with Soledad. She is probably feeling left out or abandoned. Perhaps Soledad could set a time of day for Maria to visit her in her new room.

Possible answer: Yes, the compromise is fair. Malcolm begged for the lessons. He should at least try them long enough to make an informed decision. If Malcolm still doesn't want to play when the six months are up, he can quit with no arguments.

Vocabulary Reinforcement
Page 55

Across
1. abuse
3. respect
7. sibling
8. communication
9. cooperation
10. family
11. conflict
12. resolve

Down
2. self-discipline
4. compromise
5. responsibility
6. neglect

Activity Book Answer Key • Chapter 12

Community Health

Quick Study
Pages 56–57

Lesson 1

Summary: natural disaster

Lesson Details: Possible answers:

- Local government initiates its emergency plan; radio and TV broadcasts alert the public.
- Businesses and schools are closed; traffic is limited or closed down.
- After the storm, local government organizes cleanup and repair.

Lesson 2

Summary: storm watch, storm warning

Lesson Details: Possible answers:

1. Activate the family disaster plan. **2.** Assemble the family. **3.** Seek shelter.

Lesson 3

Summary: sanitary landfill, incineration

Lesson Details:

1. Producers or catchers   2. Preparers and shippers
3. Food handlers   4. You

Lesson 4

Summary: resource, conserve, insulation

Lesson Details:

1. False   2. True

Lesson 5

Summary: pollution, Acid rain, toxic wastes

Lesson Details:

1. burning fuels such as oil, coal, and gas
2. Possible answers: oil-based paint, furniture polish, weed killer, and bug spray

Lesson 6

Summary: Reduce, noise pollution, reuse, Recycle

Lesson Details: Accept all reasonable answers.

Reading Skill
Page 58

• Screening: large objects are removed. • Chemical pretreatment: organisms that cause a taste, an odor, or a color are removed. • Disinfection: Chlorine kills organisms that cause disease. • Coagulation: A chemical is added, causing small particles to clump together into larger particles. • Sedimentation: water moves slowly; heavy particles settle to the bottom of tanks. • Filtration: Water is filtered through a thick bed of sand and charcoal. • Disinfection: final step; chlorine is used to kill organisms that might have escaped the previous steps.

Problem Solving
Page 59

A. Possible answer: The family members might begin by gathering information about earthquakes and safety tips. Then they could make a list of to-do items for an earthquake and assign a family member to do each one. Items for the kit should be gathered and discussed. Finally, the family should review and practice the plan.

B. Possible answer: Mr. Clark can explain the objective, what he expects students to do, and what the goal is. Next, he can set up an area where the trash that is collected can be sorted. Finally, he can find a way for students to collect data and report their findings.

Vocabulary Reinforcement
Page 60

1. f	**5.** d	**9.** h	**13.** j
2. o	**6.** k	**10.** a	**14.** l
3. n	**7.** c	**11.** p	**15.** i
4. m	**8.** e	**12.** b	**16.** g

© Harcourt